D0072115

Untying the Knot

Untying the Knot

MARRIAGE, THE STATE, AND
THE CASE FOR THEIR DIVORCE

Tamara Metz

PRINCETON UNIVERSITY PRESS

PRINCETON AND OXFORD

Copyright © 2010 by Princeton University Press
Published by Princeton University Press, 41 William Street,
Princeton, New Jersey 08540
In the United Kingdom: Princeton University Press,
6 Oxford Street, Woodstock, Oxfordshire OX20 1TW

press.princeton.edu

Library of Congress Cataloging-in-Publication Data

Metz, Tamara.
Untying the knot : marriage, the state, and the case
for their divorce / Tamara Metz.
p.   cm.
Includes bibliographical references and index.
ISBN 978-0-691-12667-8 (cloth : alk. paper)
1. Marriage—United States. 2. Divorce—United States.
3. Civil unions—United States. I. Title.
HQ536.M48 2010
306.84'10973—dc22   2009022246

British Library Cataloging-in-Publication Data is available

This book has been composed in Goudy

Printed on acid-free paper. ∞

Printed in the United States of America

1 3 5 7 9 10 8 6 4 2

Contents

Acknowledgments

$\mathcal{W}$e human beings cannot survive much less thrive without care. We need diverse kinds of care at unpredictable moments throughout our lives. Marriage is one popular response to this fact. The web of support that enabled me to finish this book is another. Without sharing any of the blame for the imperfections of this project, I wish to thank those individuals and institutions whose care nurtured and sustained me as I wrote this book.

Jeffrey Abramson and Susan Moller Okin introduced me to political theory and chaperoned our courtship; my first teachers continue to inspire me, even in absence. *Untying the Knot* began as a doctoral dissertation. My advisers—Michael Sandel, Jane Mansbridge, and J. Russell Muirhead—provided essential guidance in its early stages. The fellowship year I spent at the Harvard University Program in Ethics and the Professions was one of the most fruitful I had over the course of writing this book. Mary Lyndon Shanley and Monique Deveaux are two political theorists whose scholarship, mentorship, and friendship keep me in this business. Both inspire, engage, challenge, and sustain me in ways that a budding scholar can only hope for.

Over the long haul, I had the good fortune to share the agonies and pleasures of the writing process with Bryan Garsten and Peter Spiegler. Few greater are the luxuries to an author than indefatigable writing partners such as these two. Tim Sullivan and Shannah Metz helped me say what I meant. Without them, *Untying the Knot* would have landed in the trash can a long time ago.

In the last two and a half years, Reed College has done more than fulfill its promise to foster my teaching and my scholarship. Its financial and institutional support has been instrumental in my finishing this book. Equally important has been the scholarly community I have found in my new home. On this count, Benjamin Lazier, Peter Steinberger, Ann Delehanty, and Paul Hovda deserve special mention. The Mellon Foundation funds the postbaccalaureate position of Amanda Ufheil-Somers. Her work and that of Andra Brosy are the best evidence that Reed's unusual reputation in the academic world is well deserved. Both recent graduates of the college contributed invaluably to my work.

More than just the perfect antidote to hours of isolated sitting, John Allis and my cycling teams in Boston and Portland have been essential sources of friendship and community over the years. For her reliable presence, I am eternally grateful to Ariel Phillips. Liza Halley, Aura Weinstein, Heidi Dormody, Heidi Winig, and Monique Deveaux are the kind of friends and caregivers one should not go through life without.

Finally, I am blessed with a family of origin that excels at the unpredictable, constant, diverse, and sometimes trying business of caring for a full human being. To my family, and especially my mother—a caregiver extraordinaire—and sister, Shannah, I give special thanks.

Untying the Knot

-1-

Toward a Liberal Theory of Marriage and the State

On June 17, 2008, San Francisco's straight and icono-
clastic mayor Gavin Newsom presided over the wedding of
Del Martin, 87, and Phyllis Lyon, 84. Partners for more than
half a century, Martin and Lyon were the first same-sex couple to be married under the California Supreme Court's
landmark ruling *In re Marriage Cases*. In addition to the joy
that normally accompanies a wedding, Martin and Lyon's
ceremony was marked by the euphoria of injustice righted.
Mayor Newsom declared, "Today, marriage as an institution
has been strengthened."[1]

On January 20, 2009, in Washington, DC, on the steps
of the United States Capitol building, Pastor Rick Warren
opened the historic inauguration of the forty-fourth presi-
dent, Barack Obama, with the words, "Almighty God, our
father." At that moment, amid the thick whirl of hope and
virtue, on the side streets in the capital and cities across
America, some of Obama's most loyal supporters stood and
waved flags of protest. Warren's comments on same-sex marriage stirred the only noticeable disturbance in Obama's
transition into the White House. One month earlier, War-

ren had explained why, though he supported "equal rights for all Americans," he opposed same-sex marriage:

> The issue to me, I'm not opposed to that [laws that enable couples to share insurance benefits] as much as I'm opposed to redefinition of a 5,000 year definition of marriage. I'm opposed to having a brother and sister being together and calling that marriage. I'm opposed to an older guy marrying a child and calling that marriage. I'm opposed to one guy having multiple wives and calling that marriage.

Friendly interviewer, fellow evangelical star Steven Waldman pressed: "Do you think those are equivalent to gays getting married?"

> Oh, I do. For 5,000 years, marriage has been defined by every single culture and every single religion—this is not a Christian issue. Buddhist, Muslims, Jews—historically, marriage is a man and a woman. . . . I just don't believe in the redefinition of marriage.[2]

Newsom and Warren clearly stand at opposite ends of the political spectrum. Yet for all of their obvious disagreement, they share one crucial—and problematic—assumption: that the state *should* be in the business of defining and controlling marriage. Fights rage over who ought to have access to the status, but rarely do parties to these debates defend the very foundation of their position. "Today," Mayor Newsom proclaimed, "marriage has been affirmed."[3] True though this may have been on that day, it does not tell us why the *state* must be involved in making love public. And despite his own observation that marriage long predates the modern state—by some four-thousand-plus

2

years—Warren unquestioningly equates *the* definition of marriage with the state of California's definition of it.

This book challenges this widely held and typically undefended assumption that the state should create, control, and rely upon marriage. Prudence and liberal commitments to liberty, equality, and stability weigh heavily against this arrangement.

$$\mathcal{Clee}$$

In most, if not all, liberal democracies today, marriage is established.[4] To say this is to highlight two facts. First, despite a flourishing diversity of family forms and public debates about what marriage is, governments define and confer marital status and use it as an exclusive and privileged means for meeting public-welfare aims.[5] Marriage is the favored family form—or the favored veil under which to place the family.[6] The state privileges the marital family in designing and dispersing legal benefits aimed at protecting and supporting networks of intimate care. Legal kinship presumptions (for example, paternity presumption when a birth occurs within marriage), frameworks for dissolving families (for example, settled divorce procedures),[7] and material bonuses for engaging in family life under the marital veil (for example, the spousal benefits of Social Security) evince this practice.[8] Other family forms are not roundly ignored or excluded from government policies. Welfare benefits often target nonmarried, single-parent households, and food assistance is typically available regardless of marital status.[9] Still, the marital family is the preferred form. In the United States, government efforts after the 1996 welfare reform to support poor families by strengthening their marriages are perhaps the most striking examples of this fact.[10]

3

Second, to say that marriage is established is to highlight the fact that the state exercises final say over the content and public use of the marital label. Although the state is often lenient with most extralegal uses of the marital label, it can and does exercise final control over the public, even nonlegal use of the term *marriage*. Take the case of polygamist Tom Green: he ended up in jail for violating Utah's laws against plural marriage, even though he and his "spiritual wives" scrupulously avoided seeking legal recognition for their unions.[11] The state prosecuted Green for misusing the marital label, even in its extralegal form. Government wields control of marriage over and against all other public authorities—religious and secular—and in doing so serves as *the* predominant authority in the reproduction not just of a legal status but also of what I will argue is a comprehensive social institution. In sum, to call marriage "established" is to draw attention to the integral place of marriage in state policy *and* to the central role assumed by the state in defining a particular version of marriage.

To assess arguments for and against expanding the legal definition of marriage or arguments for and against using marriage as a vehicle for public policy—in short, to answer questions raised by debates that rage around us today—we must consider why marriage is established in the first place. Unless we are clear about what marriage gets from the state and the state from marriage, to what ends, and at what costs, we cannot decide whether the legal definition should be restricted or expanded, how and to whom. Marriage may or may not need saving, but until we know just what is being saved, how the state might assist in its rescue, and at what cost, we cannot say whether the state should be involved in the rescue effort.

Common views and practices notwithstanding, the justification for the establishment of marriage is far from obvious. As a practical matter, the state can, does, and, I shall argue, should achieve legitimate public-welfare goals through other means. Parents are and should be held legally responsible for their offspring, regardless of their marital status.[12] Registered domestic-partnership status—appropriately, though insufficiently—provides many of the legal benefits and burdens associated with marriage without the marital label.[13] For its part, marriage does not require *state* recognition to exist. Think of polygamous unions; these are called, experienced, and understood as marriage by those party to them, despite being outlawed.

Furthermore, state control of marriage is not a universal arrangement. In many European and North American jurisdictions, religious authorities wielded final control over the institution until well into the eighteenth and even nineteenth centuries.[14] Today, many same-sex couples assume marital status conferred by nongovernmental religious officers in many of these same countries. Similarly, among peoples who live in traditional societies at the fringes of the modern nation-state, marital status and practices proceed apace without the involvement of the state. Of course, where the modern state possesses the capacity to define and control marriage, it does and perhaps without exception. But prevalence alone does not make a convincing position.

By the measure of liberal principles, the justification for the establishment of marriage is also far from obvious. "Liberal" here refers to a family of ideas about political life, at the core of which is a commitment to liberty, equality, and stability amid deep diversity.[15] This is a theory of politics in the tradition of John Locke, John Stuart Mill, Isaiah Berlin, and John Rawls. By drawing a line between private/

nonpolitical and public/political life, liberalism negotiates the conflicting pulls of freedom and fairness, diversity and equality, independence and dependence, the individual and the community. As Judith Shklar explains, liberalism is a political doctrine, not a "philosophy of life." It has "only one overriding aim: to secure the political conditions that are necessary for the exercise of personal freedom." To achieve this end, liberalism insists on drawing a line between public and political on one side and private and non-political life on the other; it "must reject only those political doctrines that do not recognize any difference between the spheres of the personal and the public."[16] In the nonpolitical sphere, individual freedom reigns unfettered by the demands of political unity, and diversity flourishes. In the political sphere, universal norms and uniform laws govern the actions of independent citizens.

The presumption that the state should aim for neutrality with respect to matters that do not impinge on the physical and material well-being of citizens has long been central to the liberal democratic approach to negotiating the inevitable conflicts between freedom and equality.[17] In liberalism's calculus, a fair scheme of social cooperation may cost unfettered freedom in public but is reimbursed by public equality, relatively unrestrained freedom in private life, and stability in both spheres. The appeal of this approach is clear: it aims to enable deeply diverse societies to operate according to rules of justice without undermining many of the most significant differences that freedom bears.[18] Individual rights, limited but not absent government, toleration, and some sort of separation of church and state are among its basic mechanisms for achieving the always changing and usually imperfect balance between liberty and equality in the face of diversity.

Before coming under full control of secular courts—which did not happen until the mid-nineteenth century in England, for example—marriage typically fell under the shared purview of political and religious authority.[19] And still today, most citizens, customs, and laws of liberal democracies treat marriage as more than any given set of actions or delineable legal obligations and more than a simple social institution or private union. The diversely defined form(s), function(s), and forces of marriage derive from traditions of meaning and practice that exist historically and socially beyond or before the liberal state. Marriage, in traditions that dominate liberal democratic polities, was not bred to fit neatly within the limited reach of the state.

Given these facts, it is clear that the establishment of marriage flirts with violating liberalism's most basic values. Because citizens disagree deeply about what marriage is and because families assume such diverse forms, the arrangement would appear to threaten equality, both formal (before the law) and substantive (within and among families and cultures). Liberty too is threatened: because the arrangement draws the state into the most intimate corners of citizens' lives (family and sexual life, religious and cultural value systems) and effectively privileges some views of the good life while punishing others, the establishment of marriage threatens freedoms of conscience, expression, and association. With its border-crossing tendencies, marriage poses an obvious challenge to a political theory that relies heavily on distinctions between public and private life. On its face, the establishment of marriage would appear to interfere with privacy. And, to the extent that stability depends on liberty and equality, the current policy regime would seem also to threaten this third basic commitment. At the very least, a liberal justification for the establishment of marriage is not

7

obvious. On the contrary, as this cursory consideration suggests, there is good reason to believe that state-sanctioned marriage conflicts with the most basic liberal commitments to equality, liberty, and stability. While all these violations may well be justified, assumption and assertion are not adequate to making the case.

The challenge to justifying the establishment of marriage is that it be true to the two primary players in the arrangement: marriage and the liberal state. To do this, a convincing defense would include four things: first, a full and accurate picture of the institution and, second, an explanation of why, in order to flourish, marriage needs the sort of state involvement entailed by its establishment. Third, it would delineate the goods the state secures through the establishment of marriage and explain why, to achieve its legitimate functions, the state needs to be so involved in marriage per se. Fourth, such a defense would explain how this arrangement avoids violating basic commitments to liberty, equality, and stability.

It is both striking and telling that few have attempted to defend the establishment of marriage, and the justifications that can be gleaned from their writing are not up to the task. As chapter 2 shows, American jurists tend to err in favor of marriage *or* liberal principles. Not until recently did they even acknowledge the need to negotiate a just coexistence. In chapter 3, we see that liberal theorists Locke, Mill, and Susan Moller Okin have tended to focus on the material side of marriage and the instrumental purposes of marital status, at least when considering the state's role. This focus makes some sense, for it highlights those aspects of marriage that fit comfortably into a liberal tradition that takes the state as properly limited to matters of material concern—of action and behavior and not of belief and meaning.

It does not, however, capture how most, including these same thinkers, actually treat marriage. Lost in the gap between the usually implicit explanations for state control of marriage and the view of marriage that most citizens and laws actually hold is the *meaning* side of marriage, that aspect of marriage that embodies nonmaterial beliefs, relationships, and obligations and that fundamentally challenges those borders established by liberal principals. Lost in the gap is a series of questions about marriage, the functions of public definition and conferral of marital status, and the role of the state therein that remain unanswered at the potential peril of basic commitments to freedom, equality, and stability.

The confusions of practice and the inadequacies of the liberal canon leave us with the task of elaborating a fuller picture of the institution of marriage embedded in liberal traditions—and especially of the unique function of public recognition therein—than is typically offered by liberal thinkers. Chapter 4 turns to critics of liberalism—some friendlier than others—to help draw this picture. These thinkers attend to aspects of marriage that their liberal counterparts ignore and thus help fill out the picture. The view of marriage that dominates liberal democratic traditions is best described as a formal, comprehensive social institution (FCSI). With its peculiar mix of extralegal character, scope, method, and purpose, marriage, on this account, is more like religion than other institutions and legal statuses such as civil unions, business partnerships, motherhood, or even funerals, to which it is often compared.

This *explanation* should not be confused with *endorsement* or *justification*. While this account better captures the way most people experience it and our laws treat marriage, it does not justify state control and use of the FCSI, at least not in liberal terms. It helps identify the differences between marriage and, say, civil union better than devoted liberals have done but does not explain why the state must be involved for marriage to produce its magic, or how the state can serve the role it currently serves without violating limits essential to securing liberty, equality, and stability in the face of deep cultural, religious, ethnic, and moral diversity.

Feminists and queer theorists have given us more than enough reason to worry about the abusive and injurious potential of comprehensive social institutions and of this one, in particular.[20] My explanation of "the 'm' word" and of the added value that many believe it gives to conjugal unions and the state alike fills in pieces missing from the typical liberal account. It tells us what liberal theorists, jurists, and citizens assume but do not articulate and thus makes sense of the liberal reservations. It helps us understand the reason liberals would be ambivalent about defending *or* rejecting the establishment of marriage, even as it adds fodder to the case for disestablishment.

One source of the awkward silences and unanswered questions this book aims to resolve is the uneasy incorporation of marriage into liberal political thought. With a full account of the version of marriage that dominates liberal traditions, we are situated to understand the pull and push in liberal treatment of the relationship between marriage and the state. The pull comes from the popularity, institutional logic, and historical and sociological power of marriage. Most citizens in liberal polities marry. Much, if not most, intimate caregiving takes place in the ideational folds of marriage. And as liberals since Locke have made clear, there are good reasons for the state to be concerned with relationships of care. Furthermore, but distinctly, marriage is a public institution; it demands the formal engagement—the recognition and regulation—of a public authority. The state is the public authority par excellence. The public authority that controls marriage exercises influence over the very self-understanding and intimate lives of those who inhabit the institution. No wonder liberals embrace the establishment of marriage.

The push against the establishment of marriage is also clear. Although most citizens in liberal polities marry, fewer are getting and staying married, and an increasing proportion of what I call the "material side" of marriage—particularly intimate caregiving—no longer takes place within the marital walls. Moreover, liberal citizens disagree profoundly about just what marriage is. More importantly, as chapter 4 elaborates, it is especially appropriate to speak of marriage as established. Just as the "establishment of religion" refers to the state's active involvement in defining, inculcating, and supporting particular religious worldviews and institutional arrangements, so the "establishment of marriage" highlights the state's integral role in reproducing and relying on belief in a particular, comprehensive account and institutional form of intimate life. Marriage asks more of the public authority that regulates it than the liberal state can and should provide. The unique transformative potential of marriage depends on the recognizing authority's functioning as an ethical authority, which in turn depends on a shared, comprehensive account of the interconnectedness of the regulated individuals and the regulating community. But liberalism promises that stable political life can and must exist without such deep and expansive ideational unity in order to protect individual freedom and equality.[21] Marriage offers goods that the state needs (in part because many citizens embrace marriage unreflectively), and the state in turn seems to offer goods that marriage needs. And yet the fit is imprecise. The misfit is ignored at the cost of liberty, equal-

11

ity, and the health of both marriage and families. Elaborating and defending these claims are the tasks of this book.

With the institutional logic of the dominant account of marriage clearly articulated, chapter 5 turns to the task of imagining an arrangement that does better by liberal values *and* marriage. We make novel use of liberal resources for dealing with challenges ostensibly different from that of marriage. If marriage is an FCSI, it makes sense to draw from traditions of negotiating relations between the state and religion, the FCSI par excellence, as we reimagine the relationship between the state and marriage. Seen through this lens, the virtues of doing away with marriage as a legal category are clear: it would protect freedom of expression, intimate association, and cultural pluralism while enhancing equality between and within intimate associations. These benefits weigh in favor of disestablishing marriage.

And yet those who anticipate a libertarian argument will be disappointed. The liberal perspective developed in this book is heavily indebted to the insights of feminist theorists such as Okin, Joan Tronto, Eva Kittay, and Linda McClain.[22] I assume that sex and gender are essential lenses through which to understand power and politics in the world. Two facts of particular importance become clear through these lenses. First, deep, inevitable, and varied connections link public and private life. So even as I defend the need for guarding a distinction between public and private life, I am sensitive to the ways that this conceptual divide is misleading, inaccurate, and even dangerous, useful though it may be. Awareness of these connections generates constant vigilance toward the exclusions, injuries, and potential lies created or facilitated by the imaginary divide between the political and nonpolitical. The liberal solution to the challenges of marriage relies on a reformed and ever-self-critical version of the public/private.

Second, our attention to sex and gender attunes us to the facts and implications of our inevitable interdependency. Human beings are not, as often advertised in the liberal canon, fundamentally independent. Rather, we begin life utterly vulnerable and proceed through it provisionally vulnerable, dependent on others for survival and nurturance. And caregiving creates its own vulnerability: caregivers must expend resources on care receivers that they might otherwise use to care for themselves.[23] If care is to be done well and its benefits and burdens to be distributed fairly, some entity must provide a degree of insurance against its risks. The second feature of the liberal perspective endorsed and developed here is an awareness of this fact and the implications it has for determining the proper reach of state action. Neither freedom nor equality nor stability can be secured by a state that merely protects individuals from external impediment. The state must recognize and regulate intimate caregiving units to insure against the inherent risks of care, but it must do so in ways that neither undermine their norms of reciprocity nor exacerbate existing inequalities. The argument here is not so much one that flows from positive freedom or liberal perfectionism as one that recognizes that there is no such thing as purely negative freedom. The argument here does not depend on a comprehensive picture of human flourishing but rather on the recognition that *interdependence* is the unavoidable state for human beings. Against the background of this view of persons, liberalism's challenge is to balance these apparently conflicting insights and commitments in order to secure liberty, equality, and stability in the face of diversity.

There is no good liberal justification for the establish-ment of marriage. The state should cease participating ac-tively in the creation and privileging of marriage, as such, and the use of marriage as a category for dispersing benefits.[24] Still, marriage is currently the primary avenue through which most liberal states secure (however inadequately) im-portant public-welfare goals. Thus, any argument that the state should get out of the marriage business must identify which of these goals fall within the proper purview of the state and offer an alternative method for realizing them. In-timate caregiving is the aspect of domestic associational life that the state currently treats through marriage and with which it should continue to be engaged positively. There are compelling liberal reasons—beginning with the physical health and well-being of citizens and the polity—for the state to recognize and protect intimate caregiving unions. To do this and best protect liberty and equality, the state should treat this set of concerns through an intimate care-giving union status.[25] Against suggestions that the state's le-gitimate welfare concerns with respect to intimate associa-tional life are best treated by reforming marriage or replacing it with a system of private contract, an intimate caregiving union status, narrowly and carefully tailored to recognize, protect, and support intimate caregiving in its many forms, would most effectively balance liberal commitments to lib-erty, equality, and stability.

This proposal will strike many as radical, if not unwise. As a historical matter, severing the direct link between mar-riage and the state would be radical. Reigning political pow-ers have, in most places and times, controlled and used mar-riage for both material and nonmaterial ends.[26] In the Anglo-American liberal tradition, nonecclesiastical author-ity had a hand in governing marriage since the earliest stirrings of the liberal state in the late seventeenth century.[27] And yet, as recent trends indicate—Canada's *Beyond Conjugality* and the matching legislation; France's *pacte civil de solidarité* (PACS); and, in the United States, the demise of fault-based divorce, the increasing legal recognition and protection of nonmarried cohabitants, and the criminalization of marital rape—neither in principle nor in practice would the disestablishing of marriage be so radical. Getting the state out of marriage per se—but not out of many of the material concerns often housed in its ideational folds—is a move that squares with basic liberal values and widely shared understandings of marriage, and would, as a practical matter, do better by our values and by marriage itself. My aim here is to present a political philosophical defense of the shift away from state control and use of marriage and toward policies that are more narrowly tailored to support intimate care in its many guises. Upon reflection, most citizens of today's liberal democratic polities would see their values and beliefs reflected in this proposal.

Marriage is much in the news these days. A few words are thus in order to explain what this book is and what it is not. This book is an exercise in political theory.[28] It is political in two senses: the object of this study is, at its core, power in its institutional and discursive forms. It is also political in that it aims to affect current arrangements of power. And yet this study is not mere polemic.[29] Far from it. Nor is it concerned narrowly with public-policy reform or arguing within the confines of any particular liberal polity's legal framework. In presenting a model of how we might realize our shared, if contested and often-conflicting, commitments, the present study is an exercise in normative but not uncritical theory.[30] A central aim is to expose the hidden subtexts of current policy, law, and popular debates in order to assess the reasons, assumptions, and attachments expressed in our common lives. Further, the model of marriage-state relations offered stands as a critique of current arrangements.

For readers interested in American law and jurisprudence on marriage, this book should be useful, although somewhat indirectly. My argument is not conducted within the strict conventions of American constitutional law, but rather, within a broader tradition of political thought upon which these conventions are based. I draw on and aim to speak to a more abstract set of ideas—the liberal family of political commitments to liberty (via individual rights and limited government), equality (before the law and among citizens), and stability (one of the necessary preconditions for liberty and equality) as essential characteristics of a regime that honors the moral equality of citizens. I use judicial opinions to understand and evaluate liberal theory because to a great extent they reflect the liberal values and approaches that shape our Constitution.

More broadly, I aim to contribute to discussions about the proper role of the state in the intimate associational lives of its citizens.[31] And while I hope to bring critical clarity to contemporary debates and practices, the policy conclusions are the outcomes of wider aims. One of these aims is to contribute to a history of political ideas by identifying and grappling with persistent and influential but rarely noticed features of liberal political theory. Addressing the unresolved challenge of marriage serves more than a purely historical purpose: it serves critical and constructive purposes as well.

Although marriage is the immediate focus, the conceptual considerations speak to broader concerns within liberal political theory. I assume a critical view of the traditional public/private and political/nonpolitical divides—as conceptual, descriptive, and prescriptive devices—without abandoning them altogether. Feminists, especially, have convincingly shown that, as conceptual tools, these distinctions have been the cause of many theoretical and practical obfuscations and abuses.[32] At the same time, they and others have shown that the elimination of zones of privacy serves neither equality nor liberty.[33] In light of these insights, the argument presented here assumes that the distinctions between public and private and between political and nonpolitical can be useful. But to be useful, they require constant vigilance to the exclusions, abuses, and obfuscations they facilitate. As the pressing dilemmas provoked by increased cultural, ethnic, and religious diversity of many liberal democratic polities demonstrate, this relationship between marriage and the state offers a direct road into the heart of some of the most important, hallowed, and troubled areas of liberal political theory—those areas where public and private overlap and collide.[34] The line between public and private, between political and nonpolitical must be continually negotiated and renegotiated. This book contributes to the project of redrawing this line and thus brings us closer to achieving liberalism's promise of liberty and equality in the face of deep diversity.

The argument of this book takes a basic commitment to liberal values. It defends the position that the liberal approach to arranging political life is both viable and valuable and that the current relationship between marriage and the state does not square with that approach. Classical liberal distinctions between thought and action, belief and behavior, nonpolitical and political, private and public are, for all their faults, essential tools for balancing the often-competing demands of freedom, equality, and stability in the area of state involvement in intimate associations. Intimate associations are deeply problematic for liberalism. They draw affection away from the liberal state and often demand its protection. They are home to what are commonly understood as the most private relationships, yet they have vast influence upon our public, political selves. Intimate associations simultaneously demand to be recognized—both systematically, as when a man and a woman get married, and unpredictably, as when a never-married couple goes to court over a break-up—and to be left alone. (It is hardly a coincidence that in the United States, privacy law was, until recently, built around the marital couple.) Marriage is a special variety of intimate association, one for which liberalism has not yet devised a sensible model for state involvement. A basic aim of this book is to craft such a model, one that delivers on liberalism's promise to protect liberty, equality, and stability.

This is not a book specifically about California's Proposition 8 or Rick Warren or antipolygamy legislation per se. Rather, it is about the assumptions, attachments, and arrangements that make these contemporary events possible. By elucidating the theoretical and practical issues that lie behind the headlines and public debates, we are better situated to evaluate, argue about, and reform them.

-2-

Confusion in the Courts

$\mathcal{J}$udicial opinions may be thought of as societal exercises in something akin to what John Rawls calls "reflective equilibrium," whereby guiding principles are tested and refined against each other and common practices and those practices tested and refined by guiding principles.[1] In liberal democracies, one of the courts' jobs is to articulate the way that laws and policies square with the guiding principles of the regime.[2] Judicial opinions thus offer clues about tensions between grounding principle and practice, and among the grounding principles themselves.

Given that the establishment of marriage is a central piece of American public policy, we would expect our jurists to provide robust if not always convincing defenses of the practice. In fact, they do not. Echoes of the stutters, aversions, and inconsistencies of the political debates with which we opened chapter 1 resound. As we shall see in this chapter, across a range of representative cases, American courts assume but do not defend the establishment of marriage. Jurists ply various reasons for this or that policy, court decision, new statute, or general approach to state regulation of marriage, but never do they offer comprehensive justifications of the establishment of marriage.

If the key to a convincing defense is to be true to both marriage and the liberal state, as we claim in chapter 1, then it is fair to say that American jurists have failed. On the one hand, liberal arguments—or what I call the limited liberal account—tend to be truer to the facts and norms of the liberal state: they emphasize rights, and/or the tangible, and contractual elements of marriage. When they mention less tangible concerns such as education and legal recognition, these arguments insist upon the civic content and instructional functions of marriage. The justification for state involvement in such matters flows easily from traditional liberal accounts of the proper limits and reaches of state action. The account of marriage these liberal arguments present, however, hardly captures the institution that is established. On this count, "institutional" arguments do better. They tend to be truer to marriage. They present a richer portrait of marriage, embrace its less tangible aspects and institutional character, and insist on its thoroughgoing influence on individuals and society. Typical of this view are the words repeated by Justice Stephen Johnson Field in the pivotal 1888 case *Maynard v. Hill*: "It is a great public institution, giving character to our whole civil polity."[3] Arguments of this variety do a better job of describing the institution that enjoys so much governmental support. Still, they assume—and thus avoid—too much: until very recently, jurists who presented institutionalist accounts did little more than gesture at the substance of the institution they celebrated. Explanations of why and how the state's involvement is essential were similarly lacking. As a result of these shortcomings, proponents of the institutionalist accounts skirt two crucial challenges: the diversity challenge (dealing with citizens' deep disagreement over just what marriage *is*) and the limited-state challenge. The institutional picture of marriage invokes public meaning, morality, character, and belief. Rarely, however, do institutionalists explain why the state must, in practical or principled terms, be so involved in reproducing these goods.

These two types of arguments have often coexisted uncomfortably in single opinions and precedent lines, each exposing the weaknesses of the other. Woven through American court cases of the last two centuries are these partial responses to the challenge presented by the establishment of marriage; one strand is truer to marriage, the other to a limited, tolerant, rights-protecting—liberal—state. To date, we do not have a decision that is true to both. Across time, subject, and jurisdiction, American courts have failed to justify the arrangement they assume.

In recent years, under the pressure of the same-sex-marriage debates, increasing attention has been paid to the fact and, hence, the necessity of justifying the establishment of marriage in liberal terms. One of the latest decisions in the same-sex-marriage trials—*In re Marriage Cases*—does a better job than any so far in both describing and justifying the arrangement. As I shall show, the strength of the (still flawed) opinion is precisely that it understands and grapples with the challenges that the establishment of marriage poses to liberal commitments. The majority expands and refines both the liberal and institutionalist arguments that precedent hands them and then grapples with reconciling them and the conflicting demands of marriage and the liberal state. In the end, the court does not fully succeed. Still, *In re Marriage Cases* provides important fodder for our larger project of crafting a liberal account of the relationship between the state and intimate life. The shortcomings of the decision illuminate areas where more work is needed to accomplish this goal.[4]

The opinions of U.S. courts are paradigmatic sites for the interpretation of how liberal principles have played out in practice. A muddle of assumptions about the state's involvement, coupled with inattention to basic liberal principles, has led to confusion and contradiction. These opinions, therefore, serve as a starting point for understanding and unpacking the strange relationship between marriage and the state in liberal theory. Anecdotal evidence from other judicial systems suggests that the problems are not unique to American discourse and policy. For present purposes, however, I focus on American court cases to tease out and articulate the nature and possible sources of the incoherence of contemporary policies and debates.

Foundational Institution

The U.S. Supreme Court has described marriage as both a foundational institution and a fundamental right.[5] These descriptions are at the core of what I am calling the institutional and limited liberal arguments, respectively. By the late nineteenth century, the Court had articulated early versions of both.

In 1888, the *Maynard v. Hill* Court addressed the question of whether it was within the purview of state legislatures to grant divorce. The nature of marriage *and* the government's role therein were at the heart of the case; therefore, the justices said something about both. In his majority opinion, Justice Field gave the early defining statement of the view that marriage is a foundational institution. "Marriage is an institution," he wrote, "in the main-

22

tenance of which in its purity the public is deeply interested, for it is the foundation of the family and of society, without which there would be neither civilization nor progress." He continued,

> Marriage . . . is always regulated by government. It is more than a contract. It requires certain acts of the parties to constitute marriage independent of and beyond the contract. It partakes more of the character of an institution regulated and controlled by public authority, upon principles of public policy, for the benefit of the community.

And finally, citing the Rhode Island Supreme Court, Justice Field affirmed,

> Though formed by contract, [marriage] signifies the relation of husband and wife, deriving both its rights and duties from a source higher than any contract of which the parties are capable, and as to these uncontrollable by any contract which they can make. When formed, this relation is no more a contract than "fatherhood" or "sonship" is a contract.[6]

The institution Field describes is, to be sure, an institution in which government plays a defining role, but it is distinguished from mere contract by the source ("higher than any contract," "the community") of constraints on individual choice and its reach into areas of morality and character. Marriage creates webs of rights, duties, and obligations—"relations" like fatherhood and sonship, not agreements framed within a contractual setting. Its terms, though consented to by the parties, are neither determined nor alterable by them. They are imposed by the legislature and emanate from "public authority," whether the state or "a higher source." Though marriage "does not require any

23

religious ceremony for its solemnization," it does require "certain acts" beyond contract. And, finally, marriage is a creation of and for the community ("for the benefit of the community").

Even to a twenty-first-century eye, this nineteenth-century description of marriage is familiar enough. But questions arise if we consider whether this description helps justify the state's definition, regulation, and protection of the marital institution. First, one might ask for a fuller description of marriage. Which "acts" beyond contract are needed to constitute marriage? From which "higher source" do its terms emanate? Whose vision of "public benefit," "morals," or "civilization" does it serve? Although the Maryland court said nothing expressly on these topics, answers to these questions are, of course, manifest in the policies its decision legitimates. Until well into the nineteenth century, for instance, "public benefit" was seen to preclude married women from owning their own property. Second, from a liberal perspective, one must ask why *this* model of marriage should be privileged. Why monogamous? Heterosexual? Procreative? Exclusive? If liberal democratic principles promise one thing, it is that government will not privilege one way of life over others without good reason. In failing to address these questions, the Court risked violating its liberal commitments to limited government and equality before the law.[7] Third, from the perspective of both marriage and the liberal state, the Court's assertions beg another question: why and how must the state be involved with this institution in order for marriage to flourish? What exactly does it require? State creation and regulation of a contract are easily understood in liberal terms. The capacity of (and costs to) the state to create and regulate "fatherhood" or "sonship" is not as obvious.

24

The *Maynard* Court left these questions unanswered, failing to provide a convincing defense of the arrangement it celebrated. In time, this account receded into the background of judicial opinions, overshadowed by liberal ones. As we shall see, for the next 120 years, institutional arguments linger underarticulated, more often the assertion of dissenters than the full-fledged argument of majorities. In 2008, the institutional account would make a robust and much-revised reappearance in *In re Marriage Cases*.

Marriage as Actions: An Early Liberal Argument

If the early institutionalist account left unanswered questions about marriage and how its establishment might square with principles of limited government, equal protection, and rights, the earliest limited liberal arguments failed, first and foremost, on the marital side. In 1876, George Reynolds was charged with bigamy for "marrying" Amelia Jane Schofield while still married to Mary Ann Tuddenham.[8] In a decision that is clumsy at best, the Supreme Court upheld his conviction on liberal grounds.[9] The Court identified two questions at issue: (1) Does the constitutional guarantee of religious freedom make antibigamy laws unconstitutional? (2) Is the regulation of bigamy "within the legislative power of Congress?"[10] The answers to these questions, Justice Morrison Remick Waite explained, depend on the original intent of the founders (that is, did they imagine plural marriage to be protected under the right to religious freedom?) and whether polygamous marriage is an *act*.[11]

Waite swiftly concluded that the original intention of the crafters of the First Amendment *was not* to protect polygamy.[12] But historical precedent alone was not sufficient

25

to justify the prohibition. The Court had to answer the question of whether polygamous marriage falls within the bounds of legitimate legislative concern. Citing the history of the "religious issue" in the colonies, the subsequent constitutional debate, and the Lockean logic of the magistrate's power being limited to "overt acts" versus "opinion," Waite explained, "Congress was deprived of all legislative power over mere opinion, but was left free to reach actions which were in violation of social duties or subversive of good order."[13] He illustrated the implications of this principle with a telling example:

> Suppose one believed that human sacrifices were a necessary part of religious worship, would it be seriously contended that the civil government under which he lived could not interfere to prevent a sacrifice? Or if a wife religiously believed it was her duty to burn herself upon the funeral pile of her dead husband, would it be beyond the power of the civil government to prevent her carrying her belief into practice?[14]

The Court concluded that it can legitimately outlaw polygamy because, like human sacrifice, polygamy is a harmful act, not just an assertion, belief, or opinion.

The claim that plural marriage falls within the legitimate reach of government regulation because it involves action anchors the Supreme Court's ruling. That it is a civil (and not just religious) contract further justifies the government's reach into a practice so closely associated with religious and domestic life. "Marriage, while from its very nature a sacred obligation, is nevertheless, in most civilized nations, a civil contract, and usually regulated by law," the Court wrote. Just as it legitimately regulates employment contracts, the government wields final control over marriage—to the point of prohibiting some versions—because it involves actions and "in most civilized nations" is a civil contract.[15] The logic here is classically liberal: limited government may regulate actions because of their potential to harm and regulates contracts to ensure the predictability necessary for society and commerce to exist.

Elements of this logic do (and should) help justify state involvement in intimate associational life. The problem in *Reynolds* and its progeny, however, is that marriage is much more than a collection of actions or a civil contract. And the Court recognized this: "Upon [marriage] society may be said to be built, and out of its fruits spring social relations and social obligations and duties, with which government is necessarily required to deal."[16] Marriage is much more than an action-regulating contract. Invoking the institutionalist notes of *Maynard v. Hill*, the *Reynolds* majority celebrated the complex social, relational, and ideational reach and influence of the institution. Although at its core *Reynolds* presents a classic liberal justification for state action, its picture of marriage is in some ways fuller than *Maynard*'s. The *Reynolds* Court defended the government's privileging of monogamy and criminalizing of polygamy in secular, political terms. Citing prominent legal theorists Francis Lieber and James Kent, the Court argued that civilized society is founded on monogamy:[17]

In fact, according as monogamous or polygamous marriages are allowed, do we find the principles on which the government of the people, to a greater or less extent, rests. . . . [And thus,] there cannot be a doubt that . . . it is within the legitimate scope of the power of every civil government to determine whether polygamy or monogamy shall be the law of social life under its dominion.[18]

27

The account of the institution and of its relation to government may be richer in this instance, but it too falls short. In *Reynolds*, the picture of marriage is fragmented; it is alternately a collection of actions, a contract, and a principle influencing social relations. But the fully elaborated justification for the state's involvement in marriage refers only to actions. The decision does not elaborate just what the "principles" of monogamy and polygamy are or how they translate into civil norms. Nor does the decision give an explanation of just how and why state control—and active criminalization—is necessary for those outcomes. In the end, the *Reynolds* Court presented elements of an institutional account of marriage and pieces of a liberal defense of state action. Never, however, did the Court succeed in elaborating these elements and bringing them together in a thorough defense of the establishment of monogamous marriage.

Fundamental Right: The Dominant Liberal Argument

The early twentieth century saw the rise of the limited liberal argument that would dominate American jurisprudence for the next hundred years: marriage as a fundamental right, the protection of which it is the basic function of government to ensure.

In 1923, the Supreme Court declared in *Meyer v. Nebraska*: "Without doubt," the liberty protected by the Fourteenth Amendment

> denotes not merely freedom from bodily restraint but also the right of the individual to contract, to engage in any of the common occupations of life, to acquire useful

knowledge, to marry, establish a home and bring up children, to worship God according to the dictates of his own
conscience, and generally to enjoy those privileges long
recognized at common law as essential to the orderly pursuit of happiness by free men.[19]

Marriage is a fundamental right. Substantive due process
promised by the Fourteenth Amendment, therefore, requires that the state protect it. In the years since the *Meyer*
decision, the Court has repeatedly returned to this description. In 1942, the Court ruled forced sterilization unconstitutional on the basis of the claim that "marriage . . . involves
one of the basic civil rights of man."[20] In *Loving v. Virginia*
in 1967, it asserted, "The freedom to marry has long been
recognized as one of the vital personal rights essential to the
orderly pursuit of happiness by free men."[21] Lower courts
continue to cite the line of decisions summed up in *Zablocki
v. Redhail* in 1978—"the right to marry is of fundamental
importance"—to defend their decisions.[22]

In construing marriage as a right, the driving justification for state concern with marriage is clear and simple: it
is a *right*, and a "fundamental" right at that. The liberal heri-
tage of this line of reasoning is clear: liberal political theory
hardly assigns a more basic task to the state than the protection of rights. As John Locke writes in his *Second Treatise*,
the job of the magistrate is to preserve the "Lives, Liberties
and Estates" of his citizens.[23]

But just what does it means to speak of a "right to
marry?" And how must the state be involved in creating
and securing that right? The *Meyer* Court gave a partial
answer: in contrast to a right to be free *from* harm, the right
to marry is a right *to do* something, akin to the rights to
work, study, procreate, and worship. Yet the right to marry

is distinct from the other substantive rights that the Court lists: the right to work affords citizens the protection necessary to labor as they wish. The right to inquiry invokes the government's protection when a citizen wishes to investigate unfettered. Both rights impose upon the state a duty to protect individuals from outside interference. With these rights, the government's role is defensive. In the absence of external impediments, even if the state were to do nothing, individuals could exercise these rights. As long as no one else opted to interfere, one could work or study regardless of whether the state were doing its protective work. One would, of course, be less secure in doing so, but act one could. The same is not true of the right to marry. "Marrying," as our discussion of the *Reynolds* case suggests, involves more than an individual or two individuals acting. It requires positive action on the part of some public authority.

Marriage is not an act that can be exercised alone. It involves positive recognition on the part of a public authority. As Claude Lévi-Strauss writes, "Whatever the way in which the collectivity expresses its interest in the marriage of its members, whether through the authority vested in strong consanguinal groups, or more directly through the intervention of the state, it remains true that marriage is not, is never, and cannot be a private business."[24] "Married" must be defined and conferred by an authority outside those who assume the label. Rights to speech, religion, or association demand no such positive engagement by outside entities.[25] All this means that when the courts speak of a right to marry, unlike as with most of the other rights, they implicitly attribute to the state a duty to provide or ensure the provision of some sort of public recognition or labeling. This, in turn, means that we need some explanation of the nature and content of this recognition. We need a thicker, more substantive account of marriage and the state's role therein (in short, the very explanations that were missing from *Maynard*).

Ironically, the Supreme Court's impulse was just the opposite. In 1965, the fundamental right gained another layer of protection when the Court placed it within the "zone of privacy" elaborated in *Griswold v. Connecticut*: "We deal with a right of privacy older than the Bill of Rights— older than our political parties, older than our school system."[26] One important though subtle implication of placing marriage in the zone of privacy is to weaken the justification for the role of any outside authority, particularly the state. The *Eisenstadt* Court made this especially clear in ruling that the content of the union was, ultimately, the choice of the parties to the union. "If the right of privacy means anything," it wrote, "it is the right of the *individual*, married or single, to be free from unwarranted governmental intrusion into matters so fundamentally affecting a person as the decision whether to bear or beget a child."[27]

The privacy defense sits very comfortably with the liberal commitment to limited government. It does not, however, do well on the marriage front. Marriage, after all, demands publicity, not privacy. Since marriage requires positive recognition by some public authority, as long as the courts hold that marriage is a *civil* union and, therefore, that this authority must be the state, the argument that the right to marry triggers privacy protection begs further explanation. At the very least, the description of marriage as a fundamental right involving privacy protection conveys a sort of distance or negative role for the state that hardly reflects the reality of its establishment. This description effectively forecloses critical consideration, much less sufficient justification of the actual situation.

Many courts acknowledge the fact that the right to marry depends on positive action by a regulating authority by describing marriage as "a civil contract."[28] Here is yet another variety of the liberal argument. As with the general right to contract, the logic goes, so too with the right to marry: the state has a positive role to fill in that it must ensure the fulfillment of the terms of agreement. The right to marry is merely a subset of the right to contract. Note, too, the insistence that marriage is a *civil* contract—to avoid confusion with a religious one.[29] On this view, the courts fortify the state's classic role vis-à-vis its citizens: securing contract (and, thus, the system of private property upon which liberal political theory rests).

This description lacks content: just what is it about the marriage contract that makes it different from the business contract? To justify state involvement by describing marriage as a contract would do the trick from a liberal perspective. But the courts repeatedly insist that marriage is a *special* kind of contract. This, of course, reopens all the questions brought on by the underspecified institutionalist arguments: special in what sense? In what way does this involve government? Does this arrangement not put the state in a central role of reproducing deeply contested cultural, social, and religious norms and relations? Does it not cast the state in a role that relies on more ideational and cultural uniformity than liberal polities do or should attempt to provide? From a liberal perspective, the difference between marriage and business contracts is significant. The courts' failure to elaborate the difference, therefore, amounts to yet another failure to address potentially thorny issues.

32

What's in a Name? The Mysterious and Troublesome Special Value of *Marriage*

The lingering tensions and unanswered questions that littered American jurisprudence by the end of the twentieth century were slowly forced into the open by the same-sex-marriage debates. Wider social acceptance of gays and lesbians meant that their call for equal treatment could no longer be met with outright rejection. With discrimination based on sexual orientation increasingly under fire and acceptance of diverse family forms on the rise, the exclusion of same-sex couples from the benefits of legally recognized marriage became harder to sustain. Demands for recognition forced the courts to deal with the challenges that marriage presented to a liberal democratic legal system, if not directly with the problem of justifying its establishment.[30] Over the last decade, we can see the courts' growing appreciation for the nature of the challenge presented by governmental control and use of marriage and, with this insight, more nuanced and compelling responses. The arc of progress can be seen in the evolution of opinions from Vermont (1999) to California (2008).

We begin back East: *Baker v. State of Vermont* (1999) and *Goodridge v. Dept. of Public Health* (2003). In these cases, we see the courts struggling to square the establishment of heterosexist marriage with their liberal commitments—which, among other things, demand that government benefits be extended to gay and lesbian couples because they now appear to many citizens and most of the jurists as "similarly situated" to straight couples. The decisions assume, but hardly recognize—much less attempt to defend—the state's central role in creating, conferring, and controlling mar-

33

riage. Over time, however, the logic implicit in their reasoning and legal practice pushed courts to articulate with ever-greater clarity just what makes marriage special: what benefits and burdens it brings, to what ends, and why the state is engaged in its creation, conferral, and control.

Both courts ruled that same-sex couples could not justly be excluded from the civil benefits of marital status. The Vermont case produced a civil-union status, while the Massachusetts court held that marital status had to be expanded to include same-sex couples. Lost in the hubbub caused by these bold steps is a peculiar ambivalence concerning the value of what one prominent participant called "the 'm' word."[31] In Vermont, the court simply ignored the challenge of describing the special value of marriage; the term *marriage* is left woefully underspecified while its tangible benefits are extracted and extended to same-sex couples. In Massachusetts, the court acknowledged the challenges and then dodged it. The court asserted but barely filled in an institutionalist account of marriage and hardly attempted to justify its establishment.

At first glance, *Baker* portrays the goods at stake in the battle over legal recognition of same-sex marriage as the myriad concrete legal and material benefits and burdens attached to marital status. On this logic, the court could suggest that marital status and civil-union status are essentially the same: the sum of the delineable benefits attached to the status. Put another way, this position assumes that marriage is simply an instrumental status, one that conveys concrete, delineable goods (material or legal) and, at most, a generic, coincidental kind of public sanction that would attach to any benefits-bearing legal status. At least when the word *marriage* is defined and conferred by the state, the appellation carries no unique expressive value. Or so the court assumed—for only by assuming that marriage is an instrumental status could the court equate marital and civil-union status.

This account of state-conferred marital status has a long history in liberal political thought. As we shall see, liberal thinkers from John Locke to John Stuart Mill and contemporary scholars have tended to focus on the material side of marriage and the instrumental purpose of marital status, at least when considering the state's role therein. This focus makes sense because it allows marriage to fit easily into a liberal tradition that depicts the state as properly limited to matters of material concern—to matters of action and behavior, not belief and meaning.

But if marital status and civil-union status are the same, why create civil-union status at all? Why not bestow marital status on all? Or, conversely, why not civil union for all? If the value of legally defined and conferred marital status is the sum of a delineable set of benefits and burdens, then why not avoid the perils of negotiating competing definitions of *marriage* and simply use *civil union* to convey these goods?

The immediate answer seems obvious: it was a prudent political move. The court and legislature knew that a majority of Vermonters would find legal recognition of same-sex *marriage* unacceptable. And so, to soften the blow, they called the same-benefits-bestowing status by another name. But the fact that Vermonters might care about the name, and the court's resulting equivocation, reflects a deeper, unspoken logic. The reservation suggests that the term *marriage* adds something extra to the instrumental status, something that the court seems to want to both deny and protect. The subterranean incoherence in the marriage debates becomes evident. The court's explicit reasoning cannot explain the reservation behind the use of the marital label.

What is the extra value of marital status that caused the court's reluctance to embrace it fully? The *Baker* court gave only hints of the source of its ambivalence. The court's emphasis on the instrumental purposes of state control of marital status suggests that its reluctance had to do with seeing state control of this extra value as incompatible with traditional liberal views of the proper role of the state.

The Massachusetts court took a different tack in dealing with the political and principled challenges posed by same-sex marriage. In *Goodridge v. Dept. of Public Health*, the court ruled that the state's exclusion of same-sex couples from the legal status of marriage—not just the concrete benefits attached to it—is unconstitutional.

For many, the *Goodridge* decision corrected the contradictions of *Baker* by acknowledging that marriage is more than an instrumental status. "Marriage . . . bestows enormous private and social advantages on those who choose to marry," the court wrote. "Civil marriage is at once a deeply personal commitment to another human being and a highly public celebration of the ideals of mutuality, companionship, intimacy, fidelity, and family."[32] Marital status is a unique kind of expressive good, the value of which exceeds the sum of the delineable benefits and burdens that attach to it. Thus, to withhold it from same-sex couples would be to treat them unequally. In contradistinction to the *Baker* court, *Goodridge* openly embraced marital status as both an instrumental status and, without full defense or explanation, a *constitutive* status.

One might think that by acknowledging that the term *marriage* carries expressive cachet, the *Goodridge* court answered the question raised by *Baker*—the question of the extra value attached to marital status and why the state should be wary of it. Unfortunately, the court did little more than assert the importance of this extra value. It did not fully explain or defend the content of the ideals of marriage or how these ideals affect the desired outcome. The court failed to explain how state control of the status is essential to its extra value or why this special status is essential for the state to achieve its goals. Nor did the court defend the state's capacity to trade in and produce this extra- value status or the legitimacy of its doing so. Even though Justice Martha Sosman explicitly raised the possibility in the dissenting opinion, the court never explained the reason the state should *not* replace marital status with a universal civil-union status. But the position that the state properly and necessarily defines and confers marital status is one that must be defended.

Stowed away in the inarticulate confusion of contemporary debates are questions about marriage, the functions of public definition and conferral of marital status, and the role of the state therein that remain unanswered at the potential peril of basic commitments to freedom, equality, and fairness. How, if at all, can the liberal state support and rely on marriage without violating these commitments?

In re Marriage Cases: A Liberal Case for the Establishment of Marriage?

On May 15, 2008, the California Supreme Court declared that the state had to provide marital status to gay and lesbian couples. While the policy implications of the decision were not unprecedented, the substance of the opinion was. The opinion came closer than any other to presenting a complete and compelling constitutional defense of the establishment of marriage. The defense of state involvement is not the primary aim of the ruling but rather emerges as part of the explanation of why a parallel-status regime—like that of Vermont—is unconstitutional. The force of the decision as a whole and the justification of the establishment of marriage it contains stem from the court's movement beyond many of the shortcomings of both the institutionalist and liberal precedents from which it draws. Ultimately, however, the California opinion also assumes more than it defends. Riddled with now-familiar lacunae and tensions, *In re Marriage Cases* highlights areas that still need critical attention and hints at the reasons why no good liberal defense is to be found.

For the California court, questions of equality and discrimination—whether same-sex couples are due the same benefits and protections as straight couples—had been settled by the earlier enactment of Registered Domestic Partnership laws. The content of the laws and the expressed goals of the legislators who enacted them signaled California's commitment to treating same- and opposite-sex couples similarly with respect to family-formation policy.[33] Hence,

> the legal issue we must resolve is . . . whether our state Constitution prohibits the state from establishing a statutory scheme in which both opposite-sex and same-sex couples are granted the right to enter into an officially recognized family relationship that affords all of the significant legal rights and obligations traditionally

associated under state law with the institution of marriage, but under which the union of an opposite-sex couple is officially designated a "marriage" whereas the union of a same-sex couple is officially designated a "domestic partnership."[34]

From the starting position that same- and opposite-sex couples are due equal treatment, the court's conclusion that a parallel-status regime is unconstitutional turned on two claims. First, marriage and "domestic partnership" are not the same. Second, the right to marriage is fundamental. The state must, therefore, provide marital status to gay and straight couples alike.

At first glance, a liberal justification dominates the landmark case. Citing state and federal precedent, the court affirmed the fundamental right to marry. "The right to marry constitutes a fundamental right protected by the state Constitution," it wrote.[35] To those who would argue that the state should get out of the marriage business altogether, the court explained that it should not: because marriage is a *fundamental* right, the state *must* provide the circumstances for its exercise.[36] We shall return to this claim. First, though, we consider the court's development of the institutional justification.

The California opinion moves beyond the liberal discourse that dominated twentieth-century rulings by confronting the fact that, in order to protect this right, the state must do more than simply protect individuals from undue interference. Unlike rights protected by substantive due process (to work and inquiry) or those embedded in the zone of privacy (to use contraception, have an abortion, and engage in sexual practices of one's choice) or those listed in

the Bill of Rights (to free speech, religion, and association),
In re Marriage Cases opined the right to marry requires the
state to provide—define, confer, and regulate—a legal
framework. Marriage, the California court wrote, is a "positive" right.[37]

Moving beyond its predecessors, the California court
acknowledged that to defend such a right would require it
to describe "the nature and substance of the interests protected by the constitutional right to marry." Where other
courts were silent or inarticulate, the California court spoke
more clearly: it began to describe the content of the necessarily positive right to marry. Echoes of the original institutionalist ruling, *Maynard v. Hill*, are clear: marriage is "something more than a civil contract."[38] It is a public
institution.[39] But the California court added some substance
to these claims. "The right to marry represents the right of
an individual to establish a legally recognized family with
the person of one's choice," it wrote, "and, as such, is of
fundamental significance both to society and to the individual."[40] Though the court retained the language of rights, it
did what other courts had not and took up the task of filling
in the details of what that right entails and what it demands
of the state. The court wrote, *"the right to marry does obligate
the state to take affirmative action to grant official, public recognition to the couple's relationship as a family."*[41] To secure the
right to marriage, the state must act; it must recognize and
protect "the family unit."

To explain why the right should consist of *this* substance, the court identified the benefits of marriage to individuals and society. Material concerns such as the welfare
of children, the stability of families, the security of legal obligations, and the care of the vulnerable are its core social

benefits. When less tangible goods are cited, the court emphasized their civic character: "the role of the family in educating and socializing children serves society's interest by perpetuating the social and political culture and providing continuing support for society over generations." For the individual, civil marriage offers the insurance necessary for building relationships of "long-term mutual emotional and economic support" and

> affords official governmental sanction and sanctuary to the family unit, granting a parent the ability to afford his or her children the substantial benefits that flow from a stable two-parent family environment, a ready and public means of establishing to others the legal basis of one's parental relationship to one's children, and the additional security that comes from the knowledge that his or her parental relationship with a child will be afforded protection by the government against the adverse actions or claims of others.[42]

The court's emphasis on material and narrowly civic benefits is not surprising. The general commitment to limited government that underlies the American legal system has traditionally favored state action when material concerns (actions, physical well-being, property, and express contract) are at issue and presumptively disfavored it when matters of intimate life and belief, especially religious belief, are concerned. The court was clear that these concerns guided its conclusion. Civil marriage is not to be confused with religious marriage: "From the state's inception, California law has treated the legal institution of civil marriage as distinct from religious marriage."[43] Reiterating the insis-

tence of an earlier opinion, the justices wrote, "Our emphasis on the state's interest in promoting the marriage relationship is not based on anachronistic notions of morality. *The
policy favoring marriage is 'rooted in the necessity of providing
an institutional basis for defining the fundamental relational
rights and responsibilities . . . in organized society.' "*[44]

The court's concern with describing the marital right
and its benefits in civic terms reminds us, as explained in
chapter 1, that the establishment of marriage demands more
than mere acceptance, given its myriad potential threats to
basic liberal commitments. The California jurists did not
expressly aim to justify the establishment of marriage. But
when they rejected the suggestion that marriage might be
abolished as a legal category, they effectively signalled
their approval of the arrangement. To those tempted to
think otherwise and to read the court's citation of benefits
as an open door to the wholesale replacement of marriage
with a status that only provides these goods, the court
responded directly:

> If civil marriage were an institution whose *only* role was
> to serve the interests of society, it reasonably could be
> asserted that the state should have full authority to decide
> whether to establish or abolish the institution of marriage
> (and any similar institution, such as domestic partner-
> ship). In recognizing, however, that the right to marry is
> a basic, *constitutionally protected* civil right . . . the govern-
> ing California cases establish that this right embodies fun-
> damental interests of an individual that are protected
> from abrogation or elimination by the state.[45]

The court's logic here is simple enough: the right to marry
is fundamental; the state must, therefore, create and control

the institution.[46] To argue that the state need only provide access to the material and expressive goods associated with marriage—without providing the thing itself—ignores these basic facts.

While elements of the court's argument make sense, taken as a whole it suffers from the same confusion of irreconcilable impulses that characterized earlier same-sex marriage cases. The California court, like its predecessors, seems to have stumbled upon something it wants both to embrace and deny, to protect and reject: the something that makes marriage special. We have just seen that the court identified the substance of the right to marriage as an identifiable set of civic benefits. Further, the court noted that domestic partnership status "affords the couple virtually all of the same legal benefits and privileges, and imposes upon the couple virtually all of the same legal obligations and duties, that California law affords to and imposes upon a married couple."[47] When the court rejected the suggestion that marriage could be abolished, it rested its position on the claim that marriage is special in a way that does and should matter to the state. But this, of course, begs the question: just what *are* the differences between marriage and domestic partnership? Why do these justify the establishment of the former and not the latter? And how do these differences *not* cast the state in a role that runs afoul of basic liberal commitments to liberty, equality, and stability?

Like its predecessors, this court equivocated. In some instances, the court implies that the difference is deep, rooted in the long history of marriage: the marital label designates a unique kind of "respect and dignity."[48] Marriage conveys social meaning and power that domestic partnership never can. Yet, if this is what the court had in mind, it gave far too little information to justify the state's active creation and exclusive privileging of marriage and even less to assuage the worry that its doing so would violate basic liberal limits to state action.

Perhaps because of these concerns, the court frequently suggests that the (existing) difference between marriage and domestic partnership is merely the effect of the current legal distinction: the very existence of these two statuses signals difference and privilege. According to this logic, as long as two statuses exist, and especially when one has long been privileged by the state, they will convey different messages. When the state relies on a parallel-status regime, its real crime is denying same-sex couples the basic dignity and respect of equal treatment before the law.[49] Any deep, extralegal value attached to marital status is incidental to the state's concern, on this account. While this may have been the court's view, it hardly justifies the establishment of marriage. At best, it is part of an argument for using the same label for both same- and opposite-sex couples. In short, neither reading of the court's explanation of the differences between marital and domestic partnership status does the work of justifying the establishment of marriage.

Given the concerns raised by the establishment of marriage in chapter 1, these shortcomings leave us wondering what other reasons the court might have had for insisting that the state bolster and use marriage in this manner. The court's insistence that "virtually all" of the goods secured by marriage are conveyed, in California, by registered domestic-partnership status and its emphasis on civic goods lead to the conclusion that, unless the justices had reasons they did not articulate, they presented a much better case for universal domestic-partnership laws than for the establishment of marriage. If the meaning of civil marriage really is just "a legal status identifying 'family,' " then why not simply use domestic-partnership status?

The court effectively dodged this challenge by arguing that, whatever the case *might be* "in the abstract,"

> We have no occasion in this case to determine whether the state constitutional right to marry necessarily affords all couples the constitutional right to require the state to designate their official family relationship a "marriage," or whether, as the Attorney General suggests, the Legislature would not violate a couple's constitutional right to marry if—perhaps in order to emphasize and clarify that this civil institution is distinct from the religious institution of marriage—it were to assign a name other than marriage as the official designation of the family relationship for *all* couples."[50]

But this skirts the very questions that demand our attention. What is being established? If civil marriage is different from domestic partnership, how? Is this difference really one in which the liberal state should be involved? What does this extra-value status assume of those who receive it and those who bestow it? Why, if at all, does the state need to be involved in marriage as such in order to secure its legitimate ends? Why does this involvement not violate the liberal commitment to limited government—or does it? If not marriage, then what?

Although the California opinion marked significant progress in grappling with the need for a thorough defense of the establishment of marriage, it left many questions unanswered. Its success was achieved by wedding a strong liberal account with an enriched institutional one. It fell short, nonetheless, of making a convincing case that marriage must be controlled by the state for it to flourish and for the state to secure its legitimate ends, including the assurance of liberty, equality, and stability. The questions it leaves us are the focus of the rest of the book.

Marriage and the State in Liberal Political Thought

$\mathcal{T}$he courts do not provide a convincing explanation or defense of the state's involvement in marriage. Given the prominence of marriage, the importance of the goods and relationships it houses, and its public-private character, one might expect liberal theorists to have mustered well-worked-out explanations of how and why the state should or should not recognize, regulate, and rely upon marriage. In this case, theorists of liberalism disappoint. Few liberal philosophers give marriage serious attention or grapple with the challenges it presents to a theory that relies so heavily on distinguishing public from private life.[1] Even thinkers such as John Locke, John Stuart Mill, and Susan Moller Okin, who do focus critical attention on marriage, present lopsided accounts of the relationship between marriage and the state. Although they are appropriately concerned with the dilemmas of freedom and equality *within* marriage, rarely do they attend to the difficulties inherent in the relationship between marriage and the state. None expressly addresses the question of why, if at all, the state should recognize and regulate marriage as such.

Liberal philosophers, from Locke to Okin, assume that marriage should be established, and that state involvement in the family should proceed through the conjugal gate. Yet they downplay or ignore marriage's meaning side and highlight its material side and instrumental functions, particularly when law or the state is at issue. This inattention causes serious problems: it confuses the liberal case for state involvement in the intimate lives of citizens and hides violations of basic liberal commitments to liberty, equality, stability, and limited but not absent government. Care of children and partners, property rights, labor, and material resource distribution are the primary concerns of liberal theorists when they consider marriage. In this, Locke, Mill, and Okin focus on aspects of marriage that make it a comfortable candidate for control by the limited liberal state they defend. And yet, while they offer convincing reasons for the state to be involved in the material and behavioral matters often housed in marriage, they fail to provide adequate reasons for its involvement in marriage per se, though they clearly assume that it should be involved.

By failing to keep the whole institution—its material *and* meaning sides—at the center of their analyses, Locke, Mill, and Okin elide the most serious challenges that marriage presents to the traditional liberal strategy for protecting freedom, equality, and stability: that of segregating public and private matters. They therefore leave unattended the problems with state use and control of the institution. In addition, their uncritical reliance on the language and institutional form of marriage obscures the persuasive force of the position for which they provide fodder: that the liberal state has good reason to recognize, protect, and support *all* relationships that perform intimate caregiving to achieve public welfare goals, not just those marked with the marital label. In both respects, they suffer from the same confusion that marks popular discourse and judicial decisions.[2]

The history of marriage and the state in the liberal canon is one of haphazard attention and unfinished business. The relationship sits at that key juncture in liberal political thought—the meeting of public and private life—and attending to it is integral to crafting a better liberalism.

John Locke

Locke gave marriage serious critical attention, and he was uncommon even among his fellow parliamentarians for the degree to which he applied the principles of consent and equality to the institution.[3] For this, scholars describe Locke as an unusually consistent liberal, even as they are quick to note that his commitment to gender equality is intermittent at best.[4] This description is accurate, as far as it goes. Locke empowers consent and advocates equality in ways that are essential to any adequate liberal model of marriage yet divergent from the practice of his time and from the views of even his political comrades. Yet if we examine his treatment of marriage from the perspective of how the union is created, controlled, and relied upon by the political community, a more complicated picture emerges. On one level, Locke emphasizes an account of marriage that falls comfortably within the purview of his limited state in that he emphasizes its contractual element. And yet, in ways that are rarely noticed by commentators, he also treats marriage as a status, a predetermined bundle of rights and responsibilities.

Against the claim that so limiting individual choice makes his account illiberal, I argue that Locke "functionalizes" marriage, distinguishing and privileging its material aspects, especially those related to care. Thus, without saying so explicitly, he envisions marriage as something of an *instrumental status*. In this, he presents the beginnings of a liberal model of political life that balances a thoroughgoing commitment to individual freedom with the facts of human interdependency. But his full picture of marriage remains deeply rooted in religion, a fact that disturbs an easy fit between marriage and the liberal state he theorizes. Locke does not address this disturbance. In short, Locke's treatment of marriage is more complicated than is typically noted: he revises marriage in terms that make it a more comfortable object of control by the limited state he theorizes even as he retains elements that conflict with this control. He thus passes on to his philosophical heirs a mess of promise and incoherence.

Locke wrote about marriage not so much because he cared about matrimony itself but because the metaphor of the marital contract dominated the debates between parliamentarians and defenders of the divine right of kings.[5] To triumph in these debates, combatants had to show why the marriage contract was an apt analogy for their position.[6] For Locke and his fellow antiroyalists, this was no easy task. Two factors stood in the way. First, in mid-seventeenth-century England, the church wielded significant (but not total) control of the definition, creation, and regulation of marriage and held that marriage was indissoluble.[7] Second, an equally prominent view (and practice) ordered marriage according to a sexual hierarchy. To compare the political to the conjugal contract seemed doomed to favor the royalist's defense of the divine, absolute, and asymmetrical right of kings.[8]

The royalists initially prevailed on this count. They argued that the relationship between king and subjects was precisely akin to that of marriage: parties to marriage consented to an arrangement whose terms were long ago set by God, as did subjects to the king. Furthermore, royalists reasoned, just as the marital contract secured a sexual hierarchy, so too the political contract secured a just hierarchy between king and subjects.[9]

Locke presented a response unique among his antiroyalist contemporaries. One might say that he applied his liberal principles more consistently.[10] Against the royalists, he argued that the natural freedom and equality of human beings meant that obligations between adults in political society—most importantly for him, between government and citizens—must be based on voluntary consent and open to alteration and cancellation. While he maintained that important differences marked the family and the state, he parted ways with his fellow parliamentarians and argued that the primacy of consent held as strongly in the marital union as it did in the political union. Both, he asserted, involve naturally free and equal adults. (To be sure, Locke's commitment to equality of the sexes is fleeting. Still, it is central to his argument about the contractual nature of marriage.) Marriage, he writes, is grounded in voluntary consent, "made by a voluntary Compact between Man and Woman."[11] Comparing marriage to "other voluntary Compacts,"[12] he defended two significant conclusions. First, parties to the conjugal contract might opt to order their mutual concerns as they please. "Community of Goods, and the Power over them, mutual Assistance, and Maintenance, and other things belonging to *Conjugal Society*," he writes, "might be varied and regulated by that Contract, which unites Man and Wife in that Society."[13] The terms of the conjugal agreement, like those of the social contract—or any legitimate agreement between free and equal adults in civil society—are subject to determination by the parties concerned, not some outside authority. Second, he all but states that the couple might choose to dissolve the union:[14]

> But though these are Ties upon *Mankind*, which make the *Conjugal Bonds* more firm and lasting in Man . . . ; yet it would give one reason to enquire, why this *Compact*, where Procreation and Education are secured, and Inheritance taken care for, may not be made determinable, either by consent, or at a certain time, or upon certain Conditions, as well as any other voluntary Compacts, there being no necessity in the nature of the thing nor to the ends of it, that it should always be for Life.[15]

Once the ends of marriage are realized, there is no reason "in the nature of the thing" that the consent of the constrained ought not reign. Against prevailing views and in line with the revolutionary logic of his wider political theory, Locke implies that like any other civil contract, marriage might be dissoluble at the will of those party to it.

Many commentators from the period were appalled by these suggestions. Provost Thomas Elrington accused him of threatening to "introduce a promiscuous concubinage."[16] At a time when divorce was essentially unavailable to all but the most powerful, when ecclesiastical courts controlled the definition and creation and rarely permitted dissolution of marriage, and when gender inequality in marriage was widely considered a divinely sanctioned arrangement, Elrington's reaction would have been common.[17] Later commentators were also impressed with, though more positively disposed to, Locke's thoroughgoing application of equality and consent to marriage. Locke scholar Peter Laslett points to the philosopher's treatment of the family as evidence of the philosopher's unusual independence of mind.[18] Political theorist Mary Lyndon Shanley concurs, noting, "[Locke's] notion that contract might regulate property rights and maintenance obligations in marriage was an astonishing idea for the seventeenth century and subsequent centuries."[19] Focusing on Locke's fleeting commitment to sex equality and his empowerment of individual choice in marriage, most commentators agree that his conception of marriage qualifies as liberal.

The traditional reading of Locke on marriage—that he sees it as a voluntary contract between (temporary) equals—is accurate, as far as it goes, as is the claim that it squares much more easily with his political principles than the theoretical and practical versions that prevailed around him. And, as a general matter, consent and equality are essential to any compelling and coherent liberal account of marriage. They are not, however, the only measures. A liberal model of marriage and the state, and certainly any Lockean model, must also contend with the demand that the state's reach be restricted from private matters, including religious belief and much of domestic life, and limited to political concerns—to the "*Preservation* of . . . Lives, Liberties and Estates,"[20] or, as Locke puts it elsewhere, to "civil Interests," including life, liberty, health, and "possession of outward things."[21] Although Locke never explicitly defends a divide between public and private per se, most scholars agree with Ingrid Creppell, who writes that the split "served a critical orienting role" in Locke's thought.[22]

In Locke's own account, marriage violates this divide. As we have just seen, he explicitly defends marriage as a contract properly regulated by the magistrate. And yet, in one of the clearest expressions of the nature and importance of the public/private distinction, he uses marriage to help define the latter:

In private domestick Affairs, in the management of Estates, in the conservation of Bodily health, every man
may consider what suits his own conveniency, and follow
what course he likes best. No man complains of the ill
management of his Neighbour's Affairs. No man is angry
with another for an Error committed in sowing his Land,
or in marrying his Daughter. No body corrects a Spend-
thrift for consuming his Substance in Taverns. Let any
man pull down, or build, or make whatsoever Expences
he pleases, no body murmurs, no body controuls him; he
has his Liberty.[23]

Here marriage is private because it is a domestic matter.
Elsewhere, even as he describes it as a civil contract, Locke
also describes marriage as a religious concern. He refers to
divine authority as the source of the defining ends of marriage. He writes, "one cannot but admire the Wisdom of the
great Creatour, who . . . hath made it necessary, that *Society
of Man and Wife should be more lasting*, than of Male and
Female amongst other Creatures."[24] He also writes of a "rule,
which the infinite wise Maker hath set to the Works of his
hands," that governs "the end of *conjunction between Male
and Female*."[25] On Locke's terms, the deep ties between marriage, domestic life, and religion alone make marriage a
questionable site for state action or, at the very least, one
worthy of explanation. Locke offers no such explanation.
Given his concern with delineating the boundaries of the
magistrate's reach, his inattention to the details of how and
why the magistrate should be involved in marriage is problematic, at least as a matter of theory.

When we shift our focus from the relationship between
two individuals to that between the couple and the community that recognizes and regulates the marital union, Locke's

treatment of marriage looks more complicated and squares less easily with his liberal principles than the traditional reading admits. It is a mix of liberal innovations and familiar assumptions about the institution that conflict with these innovations. We might say that Locke wants to have his wedding cake and eat it too. On one hand, he emphasizes the ways in which marriage is like an economic contract: the consensual and material aspects of marriage, both of which make it an easy candidate for control by the limited government he theorizes. On the other hand, he clearly assumes the familiar, imposed, nonmaterial, and religious elements of marriage, all of which would seem to weigh against involvement of such a government. Because he never addresses what seem on his own terms to be obvious problems, he leaves tensions embedded in his theory for those who draw on it later.

The traditional reading tells us that Locke views marriage as a civil contract and that the magistrate therefore recognizes and regulates marriage in the manner of other civil contracts. At first glance, this seems to capture Locke's view: in marriage, the magistrate serves as a neutral adjudicator of a contract concerning material and behavioral matters between free and equal parties. The magistrate, he writes, "only decides any Controversie that may arise between Man and Wife about [the ends of marriage]."[26] Here, the justification for governmental involvement in this "private" affair follows simply from his wider political theory: the purpose of government is to serve as a known, neutral judge and enforcer of private agreements and as protector of life, liberty, and estate.[27] As he writes, "This *puts Men* out of a State of Nature *into* that of a *Commonwealth*, by setting up a Judge on Earth, with the Authority to determine all the Controversies, and redress the Injuries, that may

55

happen to any Member of the Commonwealth."[28] From this angle, one might reasonably think of the Lockean justification for state involvement in marriage as perfectly straightforward.

And yet things are not so simple. When we look beyond Locke's explicit defense of the contractual character of marriage, we see that he treats marriage less like a contract and more like a status—a bundle of publicly defined, conferred, and defended rights and responsibilities.[29] The power of individual consent in Locke's marriage is constrained by predetermined ends and the final control over marriage that the state wields. The internal arrangement of the marital contract "might be varied and regulated by that Contract, which unites Man and Wife in that Society," Locke writes, but it may be varied only "as far as may consist with Procreation and the bringing up of Children till they could shift for themselves."[30] The ends of the conjugal contract—here, procreation and childrearing—come before the consent of those governed by it. Consent is, therefore, less powerful than the traditional reading suggests. Inconsistent? Illiberal?

The suspicion that Locke's treatment of marriage and the magistrate hardly squares with the limited government he theorizes is heightened when we recall that he describes marriage as defined—in part—by God. Yet, he writes,

> the Church it self is a thing absolutely separate and distinct from the Commonwealth. The Boundaries on both sides are fixed and immovable. He jumbles Heaven and Earth together, the things most remote and opposite, who mixes these two Societies; which are in their Original, End, Business, and in every thing, perfectly distinct, and infinitely different from each other.[31]

We might expect the man who penned these lines to extract God from his account of marriage or to forbid state involvement or at least to explain this mingling.

Locke does none of these. And, in fact, he is not content to leave the recognition and regulation of marriage to divine authority (even as embodied in the clergy). These tasks he places squarely in the hands of the magistrate. He follows each hint that divorce might in principle be permissible with the qualification that such permissibility would depend on civil law. Various arrangements of property and dissolution might be allowed, he writes, but only "to such as are under no Restraint of any positive Law, which ordains all such Contracts to be perpetual." Shortly thereafter, he reiterates the point: "the *Wife* has, in many cases, a Liberty to *separate* from [her husband], where natural Right, or their Contract allows it; whether that Contract be made by themselves in the state of Nature, or by the Customs or Laws of the Countrey they live in."[32] In short, Locke argues that the magistrate should enforce an institution whose ends are determined by God. The conflict with his principles of limited government is clear.

Some would argue that this makes too much of Locke's references to the divine. After all, many scholars question whether Locke ever means what he says when it comes to God and religion.[33] God and religion remain in the text, they argue, as a matter of political expediency. Thus, we should not let this distract us from the liberal nature of Locke's account.

Let us, for a moment, grant this view. Even if Locke does not mean what he says about God, the references remind us that marriage—in Locke's time and ours—is widely seen, experienced, and treated as more than the magistrate's definition of it. Marriage is an institution with deep religious roots; as a historical fact, Locke's description is unsurprising. Even though church and state were wrangling for control of marriage, few in Locke's time doubted its religious nature. Still, this very fact points up the challenge that Locke fails to face. God's presence signals the noninstrumental quality of marital status; it suggests that when the magistrate deals with marriage as such, he is in fact dealing with much more than tangible goods and actions. Locke does not address the dilemma this poses to his liberal political theory, and he thus leaves the tension for his heirs. By ignoring the challenge, he buries a very knotty set of questions: What *are* the nontangible benefits of marriage? How can or should the state rely on and cultivate the nonmaterial aspects of such an institution, if at all? What are the functions—intended and effective—of public recognition and regulation of marriage as such? What do these functions assume and require of the relationship between the conferring authority and its recipients?

God aside, there is yet another apparent inconsistency in Locke's account: he treats marriage more as a status than as the contract highlighted by the traditional reading. In so doing, he limits the real reach of individual choice and consent. As we just saw, he assumes that civil authority legitimately constrains even the internal arrangement of marriage and prohibits divorce. One might think that Locke is simply emphasizing the general point that civil rather than natural law reigns within political society. But he does not make the same point when discussing other civil contracts. So even if the role he attributes to divine authority can be dismissed, the fact that he treats marriage like a status more than a contract remains unexplained.

Because status constrains the power of consent, it might be argued that this is an illiberal moment in Locke's account of marriage. I propose that it is not, at least not straightforwardly so. Understanding the reason it is not is useful as we craft an adequate liberal model of state involvement in the intimate lives of citizens. Locke treats marriage as a status, but he also "functionalizes" the union. These moves together represent the beginning of a coherent and compelling liberal approach to dealing with what theorists of care call the facts of inevitable dependency.[34] Unfinished and buried though it is, Locke's suggestion that, as far as the magistrate is concerned, marriage is an instrumental status is part of what makes his account a useful starting point for an adequate liberal model of state involvement in the intimate lives of its citizens.

Locke "functionalizes" marriage. Especially where law or the magistrate is concerned, he emphasizes the material and behavioral aspects of marriage that, on one register at least, fall easily into the category of concerns he describes as appropriate for the magistrate. When defending the contractual nature of marriage, he describes the material concerns of intimate caregiving life as its "chief End."[35] Absent here are the spiritual, religious, and sociocivic character matters that would have been widely attached to marriage in his time.[36] Instead, concerns such as procreation, child rearing and education, property transmission, and "mutual Support and Assistance"[37] occupy the center of Locke's contractual account of marriage. So important are they that Locke points to these concerns and, as we have seen, civil law—not God or religious authority—when he explains why parents might be obligated to remain married longer than they might wish.[38] This example indicates, moreover, that according to Locke, at least as far as the magistrate is concerned, marital status is simply a device by which the state ensures that these ends are met—that vulnerable citizens (both children and adults) are cared for and that those who care for them are protected. Again, absent are broader cultural or religious meanings and purposes of the conjugal status. When he emphasizes its functional ends and downplays the social and religious meaning of marriage, Locke highlights those aspects of the institution that fall within the bounds of a state limited to regulating material concerns; preserving the life, liberty, and property of citizens; and adjudicating their disputes, far from the forbidden realms of the soul, sacrament, and belief. In this sense, his refashioning makes marriage safe, or safer, for the liberal government he defends.

But this does not by itself justify the state-imposed limits on consent. After all, Locke holds that many material concerns—including a daughter's future husband—are properly beyond the magistrate's sphere of influence. What is it about functionalized marriage that would, on Locke's terms, justify these limits? Locke does not spell it out, but an implicit answer squares with his larger theoretical commitments. The relationships marriage houses, those between parents and children and between parents, are paradigmatic relationships of what, drawing on the work of contemporary theorists of care, I call intimate caregiving.[39] The relationships with which Locke insists the magistrate be concerned are those that typically involve diverse, unpredictable, unmonitored, not strictly reciprocal, and yet uniquely valuable giving and receiving of intimate care. Such care is uniquely consonant with human attachment, particularity, diversity, and freedom, but it is also rife with risk. Because this labor is typically—ideally, many argue—unpaid, unmonitored, and not strictly reciprocal, caring for vulnerable people generates its own physical and material vulnerability, what Martha Fineman calls "derivative dependency."[40] That relationships of intimate care between unequals (for example, parent and child) involve risk for both the dependent, who is vulnerable to noncare and abuse, and the caregiver, who gives without promise of like return, may seem obvious.[41] Yet caregiving among equals is also risky. Though return of some sort is typically expected, the unmonitored, unpredictable, and often incommensurable nature of caregiving means that it involves serious material and physical risk, even between able-bodied, able-minded adults. Because the risk involved in intimate care generates systematic vulnerabilities and serious disincentives, society must offer a degree of insurance against these risks if it wishes this work to be done well and its benefits and burdens to be distributed justly within and among families.

Though Locke does not spell it out, these facts do, on his own logic, justify the limits imposed by status. The facts of utter, provisional, and derivative dependency present a problem for any scheme for governing human interactions that privileges consent and individual choice, such as Locke's. Relations of utter and derivative dependency are characterized by pervasive, diverse, and unpredictable inequalities. Contract is thus an inadequate mechanism for governing these relationships.[42] This is easiest to see in terms of children: infants are incapable of entering into a contract. Even adults in relations of mutual assistance are not free to choose from a full range of options in the same sense that, say, two property owners are. Given these facts, contract—the preferred mechanism for regulating human relations in Locke's liberal political scheme—is an ill-suited mechanism for governing relations of intimate care and interdependency. Status—a publicly defined and defended identity that carries (and invites enforcement of) a bundle of rights and responsibilities—is, however, well suited to the challenges of outside involvement in relationships of intimate care. Status deals with the dangers of inequality and unfettered freedom by setting and enforcing standards from outside the immediate relationships of interdependency.[43]

In this light, Locke's provision that the demands of children and mutual assistance be treated through a status rather than a contract makes sense, for it responds to the special nature of certain types of human interdependency. By functionalizing marriage without treating it as a contract through and through, Locke presents a partial solution to the dilemma of how to incorporate the facts of utter and derivative vulnerability and interdependency into a theory that privileges individual freedom. And by functionalizing marriage, he extracts those aspects of the institution from which he excludes the magistrate—the religious, cultural, and psychological. In a sense, he creates an instrumental status that focuses on the material aspects of intimate care-giving and responds to the requirements of human interdependency. Because this status relates only to tangible aspects of the relationship, Locke limits state action in a way that is consonant with an important aspect of liberty. In short, Locke's approach promises to balance freedom and the demands of care by treating marriage as a status (conceding that contract is inadequate to the task of protecting the essential but risky relations of care) but limiting the scope of that status to material concerns (thus circumscribing its freedom-limiting potential). Here, we have the basic but unfinished outlines of a compelling model for state involvement in family life that will be expanded and developed by later liberals, including myself.

The more general problem signaled by the persistence of God in Locke's account is that marriage, then as now, is *not* simply an economic contract; it is an institution with a life outside or before the law. The awkward role of divine authority in Locke's account draws attention to problems with the meaning side of marriage that Locke ignores and that demand our attention. Still, as will become clearer in chapter 5, Locke's picture contains key elements of a liberal model of state involvement in the intimate caregiving life of citizens that would address the practical questions we face today, specifically those related to the focus and mechanisms of state involvement in marriage.

John Stuart Mill

Mill is a liberal like Locke in only the most general sense. He shares Locke's commitment to individual liberty, formal equality, and limited government. However, he eschews the very basis of Locke's liberalism—natural right—and can be read as a sort of perfectionist willing to sacrifice individual choice to "the permanent interests of man as a progressive being."[44] Still, for his defense of liberty and limited government, Mill helps define the category of Anglo-American liberal thought.

Mill is widely viewed as one of liberalism's most sophisticated thinkers on marriage.[45] Like Locke, he identifies inequality and imposed terms as problematic features of the institution. He is, however, more attuned than the earlier Englishman to the connections between public and private life and to the constitutive influence of law. Unlike Locke, he is positively committed to thoroughgoing equality between the sexes and attends to a wide array of causes and effects of gender inequality. Social norms and narratives— key elements of the meaning side of marriage—are central to his analysis. As a result, Mill's analysis, criticism, and prescriptions are more far-reaching and, to the modern liberal ear, more satisfying.

And yet, like Locke, Mill assumes more than he defends: in particular, he asserts without clear or convincing reason that the state properly controls and relies upon marriage as such, even though, on his own logic, there are good reasons to doubt the necessity or virtue of this arrangement. His silence obscures these reasons.

This silence is surprising. The proper limits of state action are a preoccupation of Mill's political writings,[46] and marriage is the central focus of *The Subjection of Women*, which marked the chronological and, arguably, the philosophical culmination of his intellectual work. One would, therefore, expect Mill to confront the questions of how and why, if at all, the state should recognize, regulate, and rely upon marriage to achieve its legitimate ends. He does not. As with Locke, Mill's wider discussion of marriage provides reasons to support state involvement in intimate caregiving but not, as he implies, in the whole institution of marriage.

If gender inequality was the first thing Mill saw when he looked at marriage, the second was tension between the individuality and privacy it requires, on the one hand, and the demands of human interdependency, on the other. Though less familiar to his libertarian fans, this dilemma struck Mill as pivotal to understanding marriage. In his treatment of it, we find both the promise and the problems associated with his acceptance of the establishment of marriage. Mill was attuned to marriage's public nature, yet he held a remarkably private ideal of the union. In its highest form, he believed marriage to be an affair of the heart: above all else, it is a voluntary union between two individuals of equal capacity and character based on deep emotional and intellectual attraction. In *On Liberty*, he writes, "Marriage, [has] the peculiarity that its objects are frustrated unless the feelings of both the parties are in harmony with it."[47] In *The Subjection of Women*, he argues that marriage is akin to the best of same-sex friendships, where each party supports and sympathetically challenges the other, seeing and engaging the whole being of the other:

> What marriage may be in the case of two persons of culti-vated faculties, identical in opinions and purposes, be-tween whom there exists that best kind of equality, simi-larity of powers and capacities with reciprocal superiority in them—so that each can enjoy the luxury of looking up to the other, and can have alternately the pleasure of leading and of being led in the path of development . . . this, and this only, is the ideal of marriage.[48]

Just as any outside force—law, social custom, even lack of feasible alternatives—would be detrimental to friendships, so too would such a force undermine the essence of marital unions. "It is wrong, wrong in every way, and on every view of morality, even the vulgar view," he summarizes, "that there should exist any motives to marriage except the happi-ness which two persons who love one another feel in associ-ating their existence."[49] On this account of marriage, public meaning, functional ends, material concerns, and state involvement seem irrelevant indeed.

And, in fact, in the few instances when Mill explicitly addresses the role of the state (or law) in marriage, he more often explains what the state should *not* do than what it *should*. For example, he argues that the state should not pre-ordain the internal structure of domestic arrangements in marriage. Though a division of labor and responsibilities in marriage is likely, he writes, "The division neither can nor should be pre-established by the law, since it must depend on individual capacities and suitabilities. If the two persons chose, they might pre-appoint it by the marriage contract, as pecuniary arrangements are now often pre-appointed."[50] The individuals alone should determine the terms of their union. The liberty of individuals to bind themselves in mutual obligations as they please, to terms of their own choosing (except those of slavery), must correspond to the liberty of individuals to choose their life paths. Mill writes, "The liberty of the individual, in things wherein the individual is alone concerned, implies a corresponding liberty in any number of individuals to regulate by mutual agreement such things as regard them jointly, and regard no persons but themselves."[51]

By this logic, Mill believes that couples should be allowed to dissolve their marital unions.[52] He concurs with Wilhelm von Humboldt's view that individuals must be allowed to exit such contracts as they choose, perhaps even by unilateral decision.

> Those who have become bound to one another, in things which concern no third party, should be able to release one another from the engagement: and even without such voluntary release there are perhaps no contracts or engagements, except those that relate to money or money's worth, of which one can venture to say that there ought to be no liberty whatever of retraction.[53]

In short, individual choice and the privacy that protects it are central to Mill's account of marriage. Given these views and his aversion to state action elaborated at length in *On Liberty*, one would not be surprised to find Mill advocating the state's withdrawal from marriage. In fact, two of his most significant influences—Harriet Taylor and Wilhelm von Humboldt—do just this. In her brief essay on marriage and divorce, the companion to Mill's early essay on the subject, Taylor argues that, in marriage, uncoerced mutual admiration and true happiness must sustain the desire in each party to remain associated.[54] In this union, she insists, the law has no place. Thus, she quips, "I should think that 500 years hence none of the follies of their ancestors will so excite wonder and contempt as the fact of legislative restraints as to matters of feeling—or rather in the expression of feeling."[55]

While Taylor wrote little else on the subject, Humboldt, whose influence on Mill's political thought is so apparent in *On Liberty*, wrote a good deal on it. In *The Limits of State Action*, he argues that state involvement in marriage is inimical to the nature of the union and an inappropriate use of political power. Humboldt's argument and Mill's response are worth considering in some detail because the exchange brings to light the weaknesses in Mill's largely implicit defense of the establishment of marriage, as well as the weaknesses in Humboldt's argument for disestablishment. A critical review of the exchange helps set the stage for the liberal case for disestablishment.

The state, Humboldt argues, should "entirely withdraw its active care from the institution of matrimony" because, he believes, it is a paradigmatic example of a relational contract, the external enforcement of which is detrimental to its very essence.[56] Marriage is founded on an emotional bond, first and foremost; it is a private union in which the state has no place[57]:

With contracts which render personal performance a duty, or still more, with those which produce actual personal relations, [legal] coercion harms man's noblest powers; and since the success of the business which is to be conducted in accordance with the contract, more or less depends on the continuing consent of the parties, such a limitation is in their case less pernicious. When therefore such a personal relation arises from the contract as not only to require certain specific actions, but, in the strictest sense, to affect the person, and influence the whole manner of his existence; where what is done or left undone is closely bound up with man's inner sensibility, repudiation should be possible at all times and without excuses. This is the case with marriage.[58]

While Mill is positively disposed to Humboldt's account of marriage as private and to his claim that contracts concerning "relational" matters should not be enforced, he nonetheless argues that the state should not withdraw from marriage. Echoing Locke, Mill cites agreements concerning material matters between adults and the well-being of children. Quite strikingly, given his extensive and subtle attention to the meaning side of marriage, in his most explicit defense of state control of marital status, Mill barely considers meaning and the state's influence on citizens' beliefs and attitudes through its definition and conferral of the status.[59] The inconsistencies of Mill's position slide through the gaps in this analysis. In the end, Mill is only partially successful in his rejection of Humboldt's proposal. On one hand, he presents compelling reasons for state action to protect intimate caregiving practices. On the other hand, this logic does not, as he suggests it does, justify state recognition and regulation of marriage as such.

The sole justification for state action, according to Mill, is the protection of individuals from harm, including the harm caused by unfulfilled duties.[60] This is his way of distinguishing public from private: individual action falls within the purview of public (here, state) authority if and only if it harms another. In all other instances—where action, specifically harmful action, is not other-regarding—the individual must be left to act as she or he chooses.[61] In this vein, the first reason Mill offers for rejecting Humboldt's proposal is the obligations borne of express or tacit agreement in marital relationships:

> When a person, either by express promise or by conduct, has encouraged another to rely upon his continuing to act in a certain way—to build expectations and calculations, and stake any part of his plan of life upon that supposition—a new series of moral obligations arises on his part towards that person, which may possibly be overruled, but cannot be ignored.[62]

This logic and social necessity motivate Mill's second reason for rejecting Humboldt's proposal, the well-being of children, the "third parties" to marriage:

> And again, if the relation between two contracting parties has been followed by consequences to others; if it has placed third parties in any peculiar position, or, as in the case of marriage, has even called third parties into existence, obligations arise on the part of both the contracting parties towards those third persons, the fulfilment of which, or at all events the mode of fulfilment, must be greatly affected by the continuance or disruption of the relation between the original parties to the contract.[63]

Surprisingly, perhaps, to Mill's libertarian admirers, he extends this logic further still. In some instances—paradigmatically, with parents and children—the state's role in protecting individuals from harm may involve forcing some individuals to act for the benefit of others. Again, the logic of social utility underscores Mill's position: because children are not capable of caring for themselves, someone else must; and because the state is society's defender, the state must ensure, directly or indirectly, that children are cared for. He writes,

> The State . . . is bound to maintain a vigilant control over [an individual's] exercise of any power which it allows [that individual] to possess over others . . . [as] in the case of the family relations, a case, in its direct influence on human happiness, more important than all others taken together.[64]

Mill insists that the state must ensure that children are nurtured and educated, for without this care, neither children—who are brought into the world unwillingly, as it were—nor society would survive, a position familiar from our discussion of Locke.[65] Mill cautions that although the state must ensure that such care is given, it should provide care directly only in extreme situations. He goes so far as to say that the state appropriately withholds marital status from couples who are too poor to support offspring.[66]

So, while Mill shares Humboldt's views regarding the private nature of the marital union and the virtues of limiting state action, he rejects his conclusion that the state should withdraw from marriage altogether. He does so on the basis of social utility and justice. Mill is less optimistic than Humboldt about the probability of uncoerced convergence of individual interests. He repeatedly shows that intimate caregiving relations are rife with divided interests. These facts, coupled with the importance of these relationships and the risks involved therein, weigh in favor of state action. "Laws and institutions require to be adapted, not to good men, but to bad," Mills writes. "Marriage is not an institution designed for a select few."[67]

Mill's argument in favor of state action with regard to intimate caregiving is persuasive and adds fodder to the reasons drawn from Locke. He identifies and responds to the unique risks involved in the essential labor of care by insisting that outside authority (in this instance, the state) provide recognition and protection of relations of care. Yet, like Locke, Mill holds that the state should not only protect against the risks of caregiving but that it therefore needs to recognize and regulate marriage itself. This logic fails on two counts. First, as Mill himself demonstrates, marriage is a complex social institution that does much more and much less than protect relations of care. Mill's response to Humboldt implies that the state uses marriage as an instrumental device for determining, publicizing, and enforcing the terms of engagement between intimate partners and between partners and their offspring. Yet Mill suggests that the label elicits an array of diverse social norms that have pervasive, self-consciousness-altering effects on individuals, families, and society at large. Far from being a limited instrumental status that the state might use for narrowly specified ends, marriage is a comprehensive social institution whose noninstrumental aspects may be its most powerful. If, as we have come to suspect, this special value of marriage is tied to diverse, thick normative accounts of the relationships it labels, Mill—and any Millian liberal—is under special pressure to defend the state's control of and reliance upon the institution. His commitment to freedom of thought and expression weigh presumptively against state action that is intended to alter fundamentally the beliefs of its citizens.[68]

The second tension in Mill's logic is that marriage brings less than he implies: whatever marriage *is*, it is not identical to the public-welfare concerns he refers to in rejecting Humboldt's proposal. He admits as much when indicating that contracts and obligations of care must be ensured by the state regardless of the marital status of the parties involved. With explicit agreements concerning money, the state is invited to adjudicate and, therefore, has reason to secure such agreements, regardless of their meaning context (though not regardless of their content).[69] But, I argue, state enforcement of express agreements between intimate partners does not require and, therefore, does not justify state involvement in *marriage*. Similarly, Mill holds that the state should enforce parental and societal duties of care regardless of marital status.[70] The obligations of parenthood, on Mill's account, stem from the act of begetting. Mill gives this opinion political weight when he argues that even the duty of care would not justify the state's prohibiting individuals from divorcing. While he maintains that particular duties to children and spouses must be enforced by the state, he ultimately concurs with Humboldt that these duties "ought not to make *much* [legal] difference" in terms of *marriage*.[71] Even on Mill's own account, duties to offspring do not, on their own, justify state control of marital status; these duties are not intrinsically linked to legally recognized marriage.

Mill's response to Humboldt confirms what the rest of his political theory suggests: that the material side of marriage is the only appropriate concern of the state. And yet he never spells this out or follows through on it. Instead, he has the state involved in marriage—the whole institution, not just its material aspects. And although his skepticism about Humboldt's libertarianism is reasonable, he leaves unanswered the question of why securing agreements between adults and protecting the vulnerable require state recognition and regulation of *marriage*. Mill may be persuasive

in his arguments about state involvement in certain material concerns that are often, though not necessarily, associated with marriage, but this does not, as he implies, justify
state recognition and regulation of marriage as such. In fact,
Mill's own logic fuels doubt about the view that the establishment of marriage is an unproblematic arrangement. Instead of confronting these doubts, he folds them into one,
tension-filled account.

Susan Moller Okin

Both the promise and the shortcomings of the liberal canon's treatment of marriage appear in the work of contemporary feminists such as Susan Moller Okin, Mary Lyndon
Shanley, and Linda McClain. These scholars add much to
the unfolding of liberal theory generally and to its treatment
of marriage in particular. And yet their accounts of marriage
suffer from familiar problems: they assume but do not justify
the establishment of marriage, and thus they obscure the
full force of their arguments and the costs of state entanglement with marriage. Here, I focus on the work of Okin.

In applying liberal principles to marriage, Okin partici-
pates in a tradition initiated by Locke. She goes further than
both Locke and Mill by exposing deep inequalities in the
formal and informal norms of family and marriage. At the
same time, she elaborates the connections between public
and private life and shows how liberalism (and other prominent political theories) assumes but ignores the contributions of the so-called private sphere to public life while simultaneously shielding those crucial contributions from
the protection of the principles of justice. By detailing how
the unpaid labor of family life incurs multiple disadvantages

in our society, how this fact is often ignored, and how a gendered division of this labor is harmful and unjust to individuals and society alike, she exposes the way that the liberal public sphere takes a free ride off the labor and injustices of the private sphere. Her critique is compelling, and no defender of liberalism writing after her can ignore it. It poses a dramatic challenge to any political theory that proposes to fence off marriage and the family from the principles of justice.

And yet, for all the ways that she moves beyond her predecessors, Okin too remains caught in the marital framework. She shares an unquestioning acceptance of the establishment of marriage. She applies liberal principles to the relationship *within* marriage in innovative and important ways but leaves the relationship between marriage and the state underscrutinized. One important result of this inattention is to obscure the full force of her arguments concerning state involvement in ensuring that the unpaid labor of family life is done well and its benefits and burdens fairly distributed. Another is to elide the threats to liberty, equality, and stability presented by state control of marriage. In short, her uncritical assumption that the marital family is the appropriate object of state action obscures the full implication of her insights: that in a just, viable, and healthy polity, caregiving and the vulnerabilities it creates must be supported by society at large *regardless* of the status of the dependent and the caregiver. Okin exposes the problems with liberalism's uncritical reliance on the public/private divide and makes a compelling case for redrawing this divide, but she stops short of articulating the radical implication of her own argument.

Okin writes that "marriage and the family, as currently practiced in our society, are unjust institutions. They constitute the pivot of a societal system of gender that renders women vulnerable to dependency, exploitation, and abuse."[72] Okin's argument here consists of two claims: first, that marriage and the family are unjust because their norms and institutional structure promote systematic material, psychological, and political inequalities between men and women within them. Like Mill, she identifies socialization, educational and economic opportunity, and property law as key factors in the system of gender reproduction, but she adds a powerful case for the centrality of the gendered division of unpaid domestic labor in this system. Especially in a capitalist economy, the unpaid character of domestic labor renders a distinct disadvantage to those who participate in it. Where material and political capital reign supreme, such labor is an effective sinkhole. The most significant, immediate effect of these socially created inequalities is a pervasive inequality in bargaining power within the family. Primary caregivers, having spent their human capital without immediate, concrete remuneration come to the kitchen table with a weakened hand in the inevitable bargaining of family decision making. According to Okin, this is the first step by which "gender-structured marriage *involves women in a cycle of socially caused and distinctly asymmetric vulnerability.*"[73]

The second step, and Okin's second claim, is that inequalities of the so-called private sphere affect pervasive inequalities and injustices in the public sphere. Here, Okin builds on and moves beyond Mill. Both argue that the deep, diverse, and inevitable connections between public and private life mean that the private sphere must also be subject to the principles of justice. Yet Mill is largely content with formal equality. He argues that changing public educational opportunities and property laws will alter beliefs and behavior within marriage. He dismisses the need for women *actu-*

ally to make use of increased education or take advantage of professional opportunities.[74] Even if women do remain homemakers, as Mill thinks they will and should, educational equality and professional opportunity are enough to alter the unequal power dynamic. Okin rejects this view as libertarian overoptimism. A systematic, asymmetrical division of unpaid labor generates unequal power in both the private and public spheres. The primary caregiver, typically a woman, simply has fewer social and material resources to dedicate to the "costs" of the public sphere. The effects of this inequality are both immediate (for example, primary caregivers have less money to spend on supporting political campaigns of their choosing) and long term (for example, over time their disproportionate influence in the institutions of public life—the paid work place or the political system, among others—translates into a public sphere that disfavors them). The end result, Okin shows, is that the disadvantages associated with the gendered division of labor translate into power disadvantages within and without the family walls. As she writes, "A *cycle of power relations and decisions pervades both family and workplace, and the inequalities of each reinforce those that already exist in the other.*"[75] Gendered marriage is unjust because it enacts and exacerbates unequal power within marriage and the family and without.

According to Okin, justice and social necessity or, in the language of this book, liberty, equality, and stability, require that society act to mitigate these inequalities through the vehicle of the state. Following philosopher Robert Goodin, she argues that because vulnerability exacerbates opportunities for abuse, society has a basic obligation to diminish the vulnerabilities that it can. Gendered marriage and family, she contends, are precisely such socially created vulnerabilities. Society, therefore, has a distinct obligation to work for their eradication. Further, drawing on John Rawls in A *Theory of Justice*, Okin notes the pervasive influence of the family and identifies it as "a basic institution" of society. Given this fact, she argues, the family must be subject to the principles of justice. This, in turn, requires that roles, rights, and responsibilities not be assigned on the basis of morally arbitrary characteristics such as sex. Finally, a just society requires citizens who possess, to a reliable degree and regularity, a sense of justice. Such a sense, Okin argues, can only be nurtured in just families—where roles, rights, responsibilities, and disadvantages are not systematically assigned to one group. In Okin's words, justice demands that the state promote a "future without gender."

The liberal commitment to the freedom to live according to one's choice precludes the possibility of outlawing traditional marriage altogether. Hence, Okin argues, the state must focus on protecting against the vulnerability that traditional marriage creates. "Gender-structured marriage, then, needs to be regarded as a currently necessary institution (because still chosen by some) but one that is socially problematic. It should be subjected to a number of legal requirements, at least when there are children."[76] In particular, she argues that the state ensure that a gendered division of labor not lead to asymmetrical economic dependence of the caregiver on the breadwinner. This goal may be achieved through public support of caregivers or by ensuring that the caregiver is a direct recipient of the goods the breadwinner collects. Generous public support for families would go some way to produce such a situation. Okin outlines one very direct method: "Such dependence can be avoided if both partners have *equal legal entitlement* to all earnings coming into the household. The clearest and simplest way of doing this would be to have employers make out wage checks equally divided between the earner and the partner who provides all or most of his or her unpaid domestic services."[77] Other methods, she suggests, might also do the trick. In any case, she argues, while the state cannot outlaw traditional marriage as a way to a future without gender, it *must* protect against the vulnerabilities that such marriage practices create.

Okin's analysis of the power dynamics of traditional gendered marriage and of the implications for liberal theory and practice is compelling. She moves well beyond Locke's halfhearted treatment of sex inequality and enriches that of Mill. If liberals are committed to the freedom and equality of all citizens, we cannot ignore the connections between public and private life, between family and political structure.

For all of the force of Okin's analysis, however, it falls short in a now-familiar manner. She frames her entire discussion in the language and conceptual apparatus of marriage. We can understand why she would stay within that framework: the meaning of marriage, as she very persuasively shows, is part of what produces the gendered behavior she criticizes. In her analysis of these dynamics, ignoring marriage would have been naïve. Still, she could and, for reasons she makes clear, should have moved beyond conjugality in her revisioning. Doing so would not only fit with the logic of her position but would have exposed its truly far-reaching implications. Okin's focus on gender inequality and marriage obscures a crucial and more general point about the labor at the heart of her argument: the individual and societal costs and benefits of unpaid, intimate caregiving labor *regardless of marital status* must be recognized and addressed if liberal commitments are to mean anything.

Okin's acceptance of the establishment of marriage is evident throughout *Justice, Gender and the Family*. Even as she implicitly raises doubts about so constraining her analysis and prescription, marriage remains the linguistic, conceptual, and institutional context within which she explores justice, gender, and the family. As we saw above, when she writes that "family is the linchpin of gender, reproducing it from one generation to the next,"[78] she has the marital family in mind. When, for instance, she considers how the state should respond to the injustices and dangers of the gendered division of unpaid labor in families, she casts the dilemma in terms of what the state should do about *marriage*. She remains constrained by the assumption that the state treats such matters through marriage. But family—and the vulnerabilities inherent in the intimate caregiving it houses—is not marriage, and marriage is not family.

Okin recognizes the distinction but never pursues it. For example, in a footnote attending her claim that laws to mitigate the vulnerabilities generated by traditional marriage are especially important where children are present, Okin writes, "I see no reason why what I propose here should be restricted to couples who are legally married. It should apply equally to 'common law' relationships that produce children, and in which a division of labor is practiced."[79] Yet it is far from clear why even quasi marriage is relevant: her argument would seem to demand state action with respect to *all* forms of intimate caregiving. As a matter of principle, marriage per se is coincidental, in a sense. She says as much when, noting that there is little consensus regarding "what marriage is," she argues:

> We must think in terms of building family and work institutions that enable people to structure their personal lives

in different ways. If they are to avoid injustice to women and children, these institutions must encourage the avoidance of socially created vulnerabilities by facilitating and reinforcing the equal sharing of paid and unpaid work between men and women, and consequently the equalizing of their opportunities and obligations in general. They must also ensure that those who enter into relationships in which there is a division of labor that might render them vulnerable are fully protected against such vulnerability, both within the context of the ongoing relationship and in the event of its dissolution.[80]

The thrust of Okin's claim here is simple and powerful: justice requires that family and institutions of the paid labor force be reformed so that those who assume the unpaid labor of intimate care are not systematically disadvantaged. Because intimate care often takes place in marital families and is typically gendered, it makes sense for Okin to focus on gendered marriage in her analysis. But the core and compelling logic here—lost behind the marital veil—is that anyone who assumes the essential labor of intimate care takes risks that benefit the care receiver, other family members, and society at large, and that in the face of these facts, justice and utility demand that society protect all those who assume this labor, regardless of their marital status.

Stripped of the language of marriage, Okin's logic runs as follows: because the risk involved in intimate care generates systematic vulnerabilities and serious disincentives, any society that wishes this work to be done well and its benefits and burdens distributed justly (within and among families) must offer a degree of insurance against these risks. As the entity charged with the task and tools of protecting citizens from physical harm and securing a framework for the just distribution of the costs and benefits of political life, the state is the appropriate source of this insurance.[81]

In light of this compelling argument for state involvement in intimate caregiving, Okin's uncritical assumption of the marital framework is especially problematic. For one, if state action is justified with reference to the material and physical concerns related to the care of the vulnerable, it is not obvious why marriage is necessary. Second, the assumption that family and marriage are easily interchangeable hides the cost to liberty presented by state entanglement with an institution. As Locke and Mill and Okin remind us, marriage is much more than a simple, instrumental institution; and while marriage and caregiving are interlinked, they are not wholly synonymous. Using one to justify the state's control of the other leads to more problems than it solves and lies at the heart of Locke's, Mill's, and Okin's haphazard theories for state control of marriage.

$$\mathcal{Cee}$$

We turned to Locke, Mill, and Okin to see if defenders of liberalism could provide answers to the questions raised by the establishment of marriage and the awkward judicial defenses of it. Given the prominence of marriage in liberal polities and its violation of the public/private border, it makes sense to think that liberal theorists would have well-worked-out answers to these questions.

They do not. They provide elements of a strong liberal case for state involvement in the intimate lives of citizens, but not in marriage per se. Though Locke often draws the limits of the magistrate's reach at the edge of the family—a man should be left to choose how to use his property or to whom to engage his daughter, couples should be allowed to determine how they arrange their family lives, the magistrate merely enforcing their marital agreements—the necessity of care for children appears to justify a reach beyond this limit. According to Locke, the magistrate may limit the choices couples make when the physical and intellectual well-being of children is at stake. The facts of human interdependency appear to justify what looks like a contradiction in Locke's treatment of marriage: at one moment, he describes it as a contract; at the next, he treats it as a status. Mill too puts the necessity and potential risks of care at the center of his insistence that the state not abandon marriage to the private choices of individuals. In Okin especially, we see how necessity and justice ground a liberal case for state protection and support of intimate caregiving.

None of them adequately explains why the state should accomplish this task through marriage, however. On their own telling, marriage is more than its material side, and certainly more—and less—than the intimate care that Locke, Mill, and Okin convincingly reference in justifying state involvement in the private sphere. The marital family is far from the only site of the essential and risky labor of care that requires the protection and support of the state. This fact underlies what I identify in chapter 5 as the target problem in liberal theory and family policy. But before we get there, we must first address the question their ambivalence begs. We, therefore, turn to theorists who make meaning and the constitutive influence of law and institutions central to their analyses of political life in order to help us articulate just what is special about marriage

and to explain the unquestioned assumption that its establishment is good and necessary. As becomes clear, although
these theorists explain the special nature of marriage, they
cannot justify the current arrangement in the face of liberal
commitments and practical reality.

-4-

Marriage: A Formal, Comprehensive Social Institution

> [Marriage] is an institution in the maintenance of which in its purity the public is deeply interested, for it is the foundation of the family and of society, without which there would be neither civilization nor progress. . . ."It is a great public institution, giving character to our whole civil polity."   —*Maynard v. Hill*, 1888

> Without the right to marry—or more properly, the right to choose to marry—one is excluded from the full range of human experience.
> —*Goodridge v. Dept of Public Health*, 2003

*R*easons beyond myopia or prejudice explain liberals' reluctance to release marriage from the hands of the state and to remove the state from marriage. The view of marriage that dominates liberal theories and practice—what I call the (un)liberal concept—invites this reluctance. In this chapter, I extract and elaborate the account of the conjugal institution that informs and *disturbs* the liberal theoretical, legal, and practical traditions with which we are concerned. As the label suggest, this account fills in holes in the logic of the traditions, explains the ambivalence of liberal thinkers, and, in so doing, makes clear why, from a liberal perspective, marriage should be disestablished.

If citizens of liberal polities shared a single view of marriage, establishment would hardly be an issue. Only in the context of deep disagreement can we even think of marriage as established. But if this is so, how can I now claim to find *a* view of marriage that informs these traditions? I am talking about two different things. In the first instance, I mean to say that citizens of liberal polities do not share a unified *conception* of marriage. Mormons and Muslims, twenty-first-century secular liberals, seventeenth-century Quakers, eighteenth-century American deists, nineteenth-century Scottish capitalists, Sicilian Catholics and Lithuanian Jews in New York at the turn of the twentieth century, hippies in San Francisco in 1969 and Gen Xers in the same city today, and so forth, hold distinct comprehensive, substantive accounts of the institution of marriage.[1] But where I claim that citizens, jurists, and theorists of liberal traditions share a view of marriage, I refer to a *concept* of the institution—a general but largely empty idea of what marriage is.[2] While the divide between conception and concept is not perfect, the distinction is nonetheless useful.

The concept of marriage that has dominated and troubled liberal traditions has three key features. First, marriage is a social institution, which is to say a pattern of expected behavior that exists outside or before secular law (typically in addition to being instantiated in law).[3] Second, marriage has a comprehensive purpose: it relies on and reproduces complex accounts of the connections between individual and community; public and private; belief and behavior; and sexuate, social, and political self-understanding. The third concerns method: marriage relies on formal, public recognition and regulation by what I call an ethical authority. To alter actions by altering beliefs, marriage, like religion, assumes and instantiates a formal relationship between individual and community whereby the commands of the communal authority are experienced as *ethical*—as freedom-guiding, not freedom-limiting. From the perspective of the liberal traditions in which it is embedded, this concept of marriage is more like religion than the other institutions, legal statuses, or practices to which it is often compared, such as family, domestic partnership, or caregiving. The latter two features explain why I call this the (un)liberal concept of marriage. While it may, as a matter of historical fact, have dominated liberal theoretical and legal traditions in the last three hundred years, as a matter of liberal principle, state involvement in such an institution is deeply problematic.

One final note before we proceed to elaborate the (un)liberal concept of marriage. My aim in this chapter is descriptive. I excavate and elaborate the logic of views, especially about the meaning side of marriage, buried in and troubling the Euro-American liberal traditions. This explanation should not be confused with justification. My explanation of "the 'm' word" and of the added value it gives citizens and the state serves two purposes. First, it helps make sense of the confusion and tensions that plague liberal treatments of marriage. It explains why liberal theorists, jurists, and citizens would be ambivalent about defending *or* rejecting the establishment of marriage. As a historical matter, other factors such as prejudice, narrow interest, power pure and simple, and limitation of imagination may well explain this equivocation. But if marriage is a formal, comprehensive social institution, then there are very good *reasons* for the ambivalence.

This brings us to the second and more important purpose of this account. It helps answer the central question of this book: should the state use marriage to achieve its legitimate public-welfare goals? My answer: no. The state does not need marriage, and marriage does not need the state. The state can achieve its public-welfare aims without relying on the extra value of marriage, and marriage can flourish without the express and exclusive recognition, support, and protection of the state. The description of marriage that I develop in the present chapter sets the stage for defending these claims and provides the groundwork for my central argument: from a liberal vantage point, the state has no good reason for protecting the *establishment* of marriage.

Unpacking the Meaning Side of Marriage

To fill in the gaps left by John Locke, John Stuart Mill, and Susan Moller Okin, we must unpack what I have been calling the meaning side of marriage. For this, I turn to critical siblings of the thinkers we have considered thus far. These "constitutivists," as I call them, are critical kin of traditional liberal theorists. Committed to the values of individual liberty, equality, and stability in diverse modern societies, these thinkers nonetheless question, often deeply, classical liberal approaches to securing these ends. Most important for our purposes, these thinkers make the constitutive effects of laws and institutions central to their theories of social and political life. Where Locke, Mill, and Okin tend to ignore or downplay these effects, G.W.F. Hegel and contemporary constitutivists such as David Cruz, Mary Ann Glendon, Carl Schneider, and Claudia Card place them at the center of their analyses.[4] Because of their attention to meaning, these thinkers are fruitful sources from which to develop a fuller and more nuanced account of the meaning side of marriage and, especially, the functions therein of public recognition. They help us understand what is special about marriage (versus civil union, for example) and why liberal ambivalence regarding the establishment of marriage is well founded.

Marriage as an Expressive Resource

More than one observer has noticed the odd inarticulacy regarding the meaning side of marriage that plagues contemporary court cases. Some, such as legal theorist David Cruz, argue that what many fail to see or admit is that *civil* marital status is a unique expressive resource. As no other label, the title "married" enables individuals to "express themselves and to constitute their identities."[5] Hence, Cruz argues, the status should be thought of as a publicly created good that can be deployed by its recipients. Individuals and institutions may intend and interpret the label differently. In every particular instance, however, the status functions as a special symbolic resource that individuals can use to say something about who they are to themselves, their partners, and their communities. Marital status, he writes, is "usable to communicate a variety of messages to one's spouse and others, and thereby to facilitate people's constitution of personal identity."[6]

This explanation of what makes marriage special adds an important piece to a fuller picture of what theorists and jurists have assumed. In the context of *In re Marriage Cases*, *Baker v. State of Vermont*, and *Goodridge v. Dept. of Public Health*, for instance, to describe the extra value of marriage (as opposed to civil union) as the unique message it conveys

89

is true almost by definition: if the concrete legal benefits are the same, then it must be the different meanings the two labels signify that distinguish them. There can be little doubt that the term *marriage* is a unique expressive resource. This fact motivated the *Goodridge* court to reject the "separate but equal" position of its northern neighbor: "Civil marriage is at once a deeply personal commitment to another human being and a highly public celebration of the ideals of mutuality, companionship, intimacy, fidelity, and family."[7] The marital label announces this public celebration and, as such, the court suggests, is an expressive resource. Liberal theorists also seem to have something like this in mind, as suggested by Mary Lyndon Shanley's argument that marriage should be expanded, not abandoned, because it is "a special bond deserving of a public status."[8]

The expressive account gets us started and directs our attention to further questions. It emphasizes the value of the public symbolism of the word *marriage* to the individuals—in constituting their identity—but does not explain why the source of this good must be the state. Cruz argues that "civil marriage, and not just marriage ceremonies or religious marriage, should be understood as expressive" because "civil marriage takes social priority much of the time."[9] No doubt, in the current circumstances in which marriage is established, it is true that the civil status carries more symbolic weight than any noncivil variety. And yet this does not mean that what is unique about marital status—versus civil union, for instance—is necessarily tied to the state. It neither proves that nor explains why the special expressive good of marriage must, as an empirical matter, or should, as a political matter, come from the state.[10] (Justice Martha Sosman's dismissive description of the *Goodridge* case as "a pitched battle over who gets to use the 'm' word" plays on the incomplete logic of this position.[11]) To answer the empirical question "Does the extra value of marriage depend on its being defined and conferred by the state?" we need to consider more thoroughly the nature of the status *and* the relationship between the individuals it labels and the public that confers it. Only then can we begin fully to address whether the state should control and confer marital status. Proponents of the expressive account are convincing when they argue that the state regulates more than behavior when it defines and doles out marriage. But they have little to say about how or whether the state should use this or any other expressive resources to accomplish its public-welfare aims. So, although true, the fact that marital status is a special expressive resource neither justifies the establishment of marriage nor fully explains liberal wariness of the meaning side of marriage.

Marriage as a Constitutive Status

To understand better how the state might use the expressive good of marital status, legal theorist Mary Ann Glendon is helpful. Against what she identifies as the dominant view in Anglo-American legal thought that sees law as merely commanding action, Glendon defends the "rhetorical" view. Law is never perfectly neutral, she argues, and it never simply adjudicates or commands action. No matter what legislators intend, laws always also influence belief. All law, in short, is constitutive.[12]

On this view, the extra value of marriage is not simply the message it conveys (which could appropriately be treated as a "resource" to be distributed), but the fact that the content and very existence of marriage laws influence the way citizens "perceive reality."[13] Whereas the expressive account identifies the extra value of marriage as a good that individuals may deploy in their identity-creating projects, the rhetorical view draws attention to the fact that laws shape identities to a significant degree, even before individuals get around to doing it themselves. When the state defines and controls marital status, it not only regulates behavior and property but also influences belief—and not just those of the individuals who assume the status but also the beliefs and values of society at large. In short, the message that the marital label conveys is not only a good to be used by individuals in constructing their personal and public identity but is also a mechanism for the state to influence the self-understandings of individuals and the political community.

We can imagine why these functions of law, generally, and marriage law, specifically, might make thinkers such as Locke, Mill, and their descendents uneasy: these effects of law complicate any approach to securing freedom that assumes laws can be limited to commanding (or limiting) action and protecting property. The effects of laws simply cannot be so contained.

While the generic constitutive power of law *may* explain some of the liberal uneasiness, I think things are more complicated both in terms of the constitutive effects of law and liberal responses to this fact. Thus far, I have described marital status as either instrumental or constitutive. If Glendon is right, this distinction is misleading: no law can be purely instrumental, affecting only behavior and not belief. In one sense, this point seems undeniable. Even traffic laws, perhaps the paradigmatic example of instrumental rules, alter the way we perceive reality. No doubt they cultivate in many people deep, unthinking reactions to their symbols: stopping at a stop sign is for most individuals a semiconscious response. Instrumental laws may even promote a feeling of trust among citizens and in government. In this broad sense, then, Glendon's claim that the effects of law are never limited to the behavioral is irrefutable. No reasonable thinker—including Locke, Mill, and Okin—could deny this (although they might ignore or downplay it).

And yet, the claim that all laws in some way influence the way we see things elides critical differences between the constitutive purposes and effects of, say, traffic laws and those of marriage laws. Even if we could admit that serious social meaning attaches to a driver's license, for instance, no one would tout that as a basic purpose of that status. No one, that is, would worry about the extralegal use of "the 'd' word," so long as it was not being used to hide illegal *actions*. The fact that public use of "the 'm' word" is at the center of many of today's marriage battles is, therefore, significant. No matter what influence traffic laws have on the self-understandings of citizens, it makes little sense to say that the primary purpose or effect of these laws is to cultivate those self-understandings. These laws command behavior and only *incidentally* alter belief.

Marriage laws, on the other hand, are often described by jurists and contemporary commentators as essential means for cultivating citizen character. Presaging the *Maynard v. Hill* decision, the majority of *Reynolds v. United States* wrote: "Upon it society may be said to be built, and out of its fruits spring social relations and social obligations and duties, with which government is necessarily required to deal."[14] On this view, a basic function—purpose and effect—of these laws is to alter self-understanding. On widely held views, anyway, the functions of marriage laws extend beyond the material and incidentally constitutive. Commentator Jonathan Rauch elaborates: "Marriage does much more than ratify relationships . . . ; it fortifies relationships by embedding them in a dense web of social expectations. That is why marriage, with or without children, is a win-win deal, strengthening individuals, families, and communities all at the same time."[15] So even though both traffic and marriage laws are, in some sense, constitutive, it is reasonable to distinguish between their belief-altering purposes and effects. Clearly, there is something else about marriage laws, beyond their generic constitutive potential, that invites the state's jealous if ambivalent and inadequate defense of its control over the public definition and use of the status.

To elaborate the differences between the meaning sides of marriage and driving laws, we can start with—but then must move beyond—Glendon's insight that all law is constitutive. In deference to her insights, we will call laws such as traffic rules, concerned primarily with regulating action and material matters, *instrumental.* They alter self-understanding as an incidental effect. In contrast, I will call marriage laws *hyperconstitutive* laws, for meaning cultivation and belief formation are their integral functions.

Marriage as a Social Institution

If Vermont's *civil union* is an instrumental status and its *marriage* a hyperconstitutive one—though they convey the same material benefits and legal protections and both, admittedly, have some constitutive effect—what is the source of the difference? The answer lies outside the law, in the extralegal institution with which marital status is associated. Through this association, the state gains access to purposes and powers that extend beyond those expressed in the letter of the law. Here, we can begin fully to appreciate why the state is both ready and reluctant to relinquish its control over the definition, regulation, and use of marriage.

Recall, from chapter 2, that U.S. courts often point to "the institution" of marriage to explain their rulings. "This case implicates the public institution of marriage, an institution the law protects," wrote *Utah v. Holm.*[16] What does it mean for the state to defend the "institution of marriage"? Why and how is this end achieved? Beyond regulating actions and property, what does this feat involve? Why would the extralegal use of the marital label jeopardize marriage or the state's accomplishment of its legitimate public-welfare goals? What does the institutionalist defense assume about marriage and the state?

In explaining how law and social institutions interact to the advantage of both, theorists Carl Schneider and Claudia Card answer these questions and, in so doing, help round out our description of the institutionalist account of marriage we first saw in the courts' writing. The extra value of the civil status of marriage has everything to do with *marriage*—the socially significant (if variously defined) "pattern of expected action" that, in various senses, preexists legal definition and regulation. What makes marriage different from civil union has little to do with legal definitions or concrete benefits and much to do with the extralegal social institution that shares its name. In bolstering these institutions and tying them to the state, the association makes available to the state decidedly extralegal powers and spheres of influence, entanglement with which the state need not admit.

Schneider describes "channeling" as the process by which law funnels people into social institutions, "a pattern of expected action of individuals or groups enforced by social sanctions, both positive and negative."[17] Three aspects of his description are useful for our purposes. First, social institutions exist independent of, before, or outside the state. Though the state may bolster these "patterns of behavior" by directing resources and recognition their way, the institutions predate, as it were, the state. Second, social institutions consist of and are concerned with both behavior *and* meaning. Social institutions are, rather crudely, patterns of behavior explained and promoted by a socially significant story. Third, the strictures of social institutions, in contrast to those of the state, are more likely to be experienced as "natural."[18] Citing marriage and motherhood as paradigmatic examples of social institutions with which channeling is often and effectively used, Schneider argues that channeling "relies centrally but not exclusively on social approval of the institution, on social rewards for its use, and on social disfavor of its alternatives. . . .The law may buttress an institution here and harry its competitors there. But . . . 'the primary social control is given in the existence of an institution as such.' "[19]

On this account, the state and preexisting social institutions complement and empower each other. The benefits to the institutions are perhaps obvious. By recognizing and endorsing related statuses and rewarding and punishing for use and nonuse, the state encourages citizens to participate in, and thereby bolsters, its favored institutions.[20]

The benefits to the state may seem less obvious but are, in fact, significant in two areas: purposes and powers. Through this interdependence, the state makes use of and reinforces purposes not delineated in the letter of the law; these are the purposes that are part of the story by which the behavior is patterned and from which it derives its meaning. Even if marriage law regulates only behavior, the civil status, through its association with the social institution, extends its aims and effects to belief and social norms. Thus, feminists and queer theorists including Mill, Okin, Drucilla Cornell, Michael Warner, and Claudia Card have shown that, through marriage, the state extends the scope of its control well beyond material or otherwise public concerns. Marriage conveys, enforces, and privileges standards of normality regarding what Cornell calls the "sexuate being"—"the sexed body of our human being when engaged with a framework by which we orient ourselves; because we are sexuate beings we have to orient ourselves sexually."[21] By drawing on and bolstering dominant social norms, marriage is the "pivot" of systems of gender and sexual normalization.[22] Thus, through its association with the social institution of marriage, the purpose and reach of the legal status are extended beyond those delineated in its express language. Both in terms of purpose (altering behavior *and* belief) and scope (sexuate to political identity), the civil status assumes comprehensive purposes and concerns.

Perhaps even more significant than its expanded purposes is the access the state gains to extralegal sources of power—motivation and authority. Its association with the preexisting social institution gives *civil* marriage—and, therefore, the state—*uncivil* means of constraining and cultivating citizen behavior and belief. By participating in a social institution, the state accesses and bolsters the naturalizing function of social norms. Extralegal norms and related pressures and expectations, comprehensive moral and cultural doctrines, and their unique power to train behavior *and* belief all become available to the state in its association with social institutions such as marriage. As I shall elaborate below with Hegel's help, the importance of the state's access to this type of power cannot be underestimated. Compared to the unadorned commands of the state, these strictures have the unique characteristic of often being experienced as so "natural" as to be unrecognizable strictures at all.[23]

The state recognizes and regulates marriage as such because it is the institution with which the state is concerned, and not its component parts—the various goods and relationships it often houses. As the *Holm* court asserts but fails to defend fully, the state could not replace marriage with civil union without significant costs. No matter how civil union is defined, no matter what concrete benefits it carries, it cannot draw on the same social, cultural, and emotional associations and histories upon which marriage draws. This is not to say that civil union would not, over time, develop its own existence as a social institution or that it could not draw illicitly on norms of marriage; but never would it have the same integral ties to the varieties of marriage that populate the sociocultural map of society and, therefore, to their unique powers. At the same time, the fully elaborated institutionalist story helps explain why courts would be wary of expressly defending this stance. By recognizing and regulating marriage as such, the state somewhat extends its purposes, scope, and powers beyond those delineated in the law and in ways unavailable through other civil statuses. It is here, I shall argue, where the unacknowledged problems with the establishment of marriage lie.

Marriage as a Formal Social Institution

To appreciate the nature of the problems buried here, we need to add a final piece to our picture of the meaning side of marriage, a fuller explanation of the nature and institutional significance of *formal public recognition* of marriage. We need to be able to explain, in concrete terms, the state's obsession with keeping *marriage*, "the 'm' word," out of the hands of the polygamists. What explains the fact that the state is willing to punish even the nonlegal use of the label?

The answer lies in the distinction between informal and formal social institutions. Both Card and Schneider use marriage and motherhood to illustrate their arguments about how a legal institution makes use of and bolsters social norms.[24] The coincidence is striking because, for all their similarities, marriage and motherhood have one very obvious and, from our perspective, very relevant difference: marriage requires formal public involvement in a way that motherhood does not. If motherhood is a social institution in the terms just outlined—a roughly identifiable set of pre-legal practices, embedded in (variously defined) social narratives that make its constraints and benefits experienced as almost natural—marriage is a *formal* social institution. Motherhood exists without formal public recognition. Without denying the important role social norms and even legal status have in defining motherhood, we can nonetheless say that, in some straightforward sense, motherhood exists without any formal public recognition. A woman can be a mother—in some recognizable sense—without asking any public authority for its sanction.

Marriage, in contrast to motherhood, requires the formal involvement of a public authority to exist. (This authority need not—and if we care about marriage, intimate care, liberty, equality, and stability, ought not—be the *state*.) Formal public control—recognition and regulation—is essential to the purposes and powers of the institution in a way that is unmatched by the logic of an informal social institution such as motherhood. The need for formal recognition of marriage creates a more direct avenue into the beliefs and behaviors it encompasses than does the lack therein of motherhood. In addition, because of the integral place of public recognition in marriage the control wielded by the external authority is at least qualitatively distinct from that of motherhood, if not also more powerful. Public meaning, created and conveyed through public control, is a primary good and function of this institution. Hence, the authority that defines, confers, and regulates the label controls the institution and its powers. For these reasons, I propose that the state is loath to relinquish control of marriage and its label, even as it often hesitates to defend this control. The threat posed by polygamists' extralegal use of the label, on this account, is that it stands to fragment and decentralize both the singular meaning of and source of authority in the institution. The function of formal public recognition concentrates power in the label *marriage* in a manner unmatched by the term *mother*. This difference helps explain why one might think marriage needs the state's imprimatur to flourish in a way that motherhood does not. The difference between formal and informal institutions helps explain why the establishment of marriage but not of motherhood is possible.

To help elaborate the nature and significance of this difference, we turn to Hegel.[25] He paints a picture of the psychosocial dynamics of marriage and of the functions of public recognition and regulation of marriage that shows how public control of marital status can, under the right conditions, serve as a uniquely powerful means of integrating individuals and the conferring community. In this, Hegel helps illustrate with unusual clarity the dangers—from a liberal perspective—of state control of marriage.[26]

Like the liberal theorists we considered in chapter 3, Hegel describes marriage as a contract and then some. Unlike his liberal counterparts, however, when Hegel looks at marriage, inequality and consent are not the challenges he sees. Rather, he sees the challenge of and solution to unmitigated separateness—of individuals from/to each other and of individuals from/to society as a whole. For Hegel, the great virtue of marriage is what it does: it integrates individuals with each other and with their community and its norms, practices, and institutions, so that their inevitable interdependence is experienced as natural and thus, in some sense, not constraining. In this, beyond its very important instrumental functions—governing express agreements and regulating action and material matters—Hegel explains that marriage serves what we earlier called a hyperconstitutive function: it trains individuals to see themselves as organically tied to social and political institutions and attendant belief systems.[27] Here, he echoes (and extends the logic of) Schneider's and Card's explanations of marriage's social-psychological powers. For our purposes, however, Hegel's most important contribution to our investigation is his description of *how* marriage accomplishes this feat of thoroughgoing integration. By explaining why formal public recognition is so central to the purposes and effects of marriage, Hegel adds the final piece to our puzzle—the picture of marriage that is assumed but not fully elaborated in liberals' treatment of the institution.

According to Hegel, marriage integrates the individual and community and fosters the conditions for freedom by reconstituting the self-understanding of those in its ideational and material-legal folds. Marriage, therefore, forms the bedrock of free society.[28] Hegel calls marriage a "contract to transcend the standpoint of contract."[29] The key to this transcendence, for Hegel, lies in the formal, public control over and involvement in the institution. The key to achieving the interpersonal and social integration that draws marriage beyond its contractual origins is more than the expressive value of the status or its generic constitutive powers or its characteristics as a social institution: it is the formal involvement by an ethical authority.

To understand Hegel's argument, it is useful to consider the role he assigns public authority in economic contracts. According to Hegel, the external authority in the economic contract provides a limited type of security—the threat of forceful punishment or repayment upon nonfulfillment. Public involvement here is distant, legalistic, and neutral, present more often in its absence.[30] To be sure, shared understandings of the meaning and validity of contract must preexist the act itself.[31] As this distant role of the recognizing authority suggests, the story it assumes, in particular the story about the relationship between community and contractors, is one about objects that can be alienated. Part of the shared understanding of contract is precisely its limited reach and purposes and the related limited role of the external authority. Sealing a commercial contract, however, requires neither a public ceremonial performance nor the direct involvement of an ethical authority.

In the conjugal contract, on the other hand, the public's involvement is substantive, intimate, and *ethical*. Whereas an economic contract can be concluded with only the verbal exchange of vows between two people,[32] the marriage contract requires, in addition, the explicit sanction of outside entities. The "ethical" moment of marriage, according to Hegel, comes into being and has compelling force only when the individuals formally and expressly consent to the terms of marriage, when they self-consciously acknowledge their entrance into the institution and its norms of behavior (which although apparently self-restricting are also liberating) in the announced presence of the community that determines those terms and norms. "The solemn declaration by the parties of their consent to enter the ethical bond of marriage, and its corresponding recognition and confirmation by their family and community,[33] constitutes the formal completion and actuality of marriage," writes Hegel.[34] The public celebration, or "solemn declaration" in front of others, is a pivotal point in the movement from contract to transcendence. The community's involvement enacts the message that marriage both depends on and derives meaning from the communal context in which it is embedded.

The third recognizing party is involved not merely as a legal check but as an "ethical authority"[35]—an authority whose directives are experienced as natural and freedom-guiding, not freedom-limiting, by dint of the shared view of the relationship between the individual and the community of which this authority is a representative. Here, a religious example is illuminating: to a believing Catholic, the pope's commands are freedom-guiding, in that Catholics believe that the pontiff's commands guide them to some freedom or good beyond that which they can currently perceive. Effective ethical authority assumes shared understandings about the nature of the relationship it labels and, crucially, about the appropriateness of that authority's commands in matters of the most intimate nature, including belief. If the recognizing authority is seen only as expressing legal authority—as the state does in a civil union, for instance—then marriage loses its special integrating power and becomes little more than a contract or, at most, to use our terms, an instrumental status. As Hegel writes,

> If this ceremony is taken as an external formality, a mere so-called "civil requirement," it is thereby stripped of all significance except perhaps that of serving the purpose of edification and attesting the civil relation of the parties. It is reduced indeed to a mere *fiat* of a civil or ecclesiastical authority. As such it appears as something not merely in-

different to the true nature of marriage, but actually alien to it. The heart is constrained by the law to attach a value to the formal ceremony and the latter is looked upon merely as a condition which must precede the complete mutual surrender of the parties to one another. . . .[This] view just criticized casts aside marriage's specifically ethical character.[36]

According to Hegel, everyone involved must understand marriage as more than a simple contract or an instrumental legal status for marriage to transcend its contractual starting point. The institution requires a higher or expanded meaning derived from its place in a comprehensive story about the relationship between intimate associational and political life, freedom as their integration, and the freedom-guiding nature of the recognizing authority and the scheme of freedom. This meaning is transmitted through, symbolized, and actualized in the public's definition, conferral, and regulation of marriage status.

Hegel's view of the nature and importance of the recognizing public function as an ethical authority is especially clear when he discusses divorce. Despite his aversion to "ought" commands, Hegel comes quite close to producing one on the subject of divorce. Because marriage is an ethical matter and because it is meant to provide a safe haven for mutual interdependence, the union ought to be indissoluble. Since the union is based on subjective feeling, however, it must also be dissoluble. Hegel resolves what might seem an insurmountable quandary with the help of the ethical authority. "To be sure," he argues, "marriage *ought* to be indissoluble, but here again we have to stop at this 'ought'; yet, since marriage is an ethical institution, it cannot be dissolved at will but only by an ethical authority, whether the church or the law-court."[37] Although divorce must be available to those who find themselves totally estranged (so that subjective will might be respected), only an outside ethical authority can grant it. It must be an ethical authority in order to maintain the respect for the individual will. Since the difference between a freedom-limiting and a freedom-guiding command is a matter of what the commanded believes about the commander, there must be a shared vision of the relationship between individuals and their community for ethical authority to exist.

What makes marriage different from a complex social institution like motherhood and an instrumental status like civil union? Like the constitutivists, Hegel points to both purpose and method. On the former, he echoes (and extends) the insights of the institutionalists by identifying comprehensive integration as the overriding purpose of marriage. Unlike an instrumental status, aimed at regulating material matters, property, and behavior, marriage aims to integrate spouses with one another and individuals with their community from *within*, from the most private beliefs about sexuate being to the most public behaviors related to property. Hegel most significantly adds to our description of the meaning side of marriage in his explanation of *how* marriage achieves this feat. Through the formal, public definition and regulation of an intimate union by an ethical authority, that union is transformed into a *marital* union. Marriage is a public creation, an invention of the community that defines and confers the status. Friendships and intimate partnerships can exist without the express or formal recognition of anyone outside the individuals involved. Marriage cannot.[38]

Like contracts and any formal public status, the marital institution and individual marriages exist by dint of their formal recognition, definition, and dispersal by a community. But unlike contract and many other public statuses, marriage relies upon and reproduces ethical authority. Both marriage and instrumental statuses might regulate intimate, sexual behavior, but only marriage openly invites regulation and cultivation of beliefs. Marriage aims to alter the self-understanding, affective attachments and inclinations, norms, and expectations of those it covers in its ideational folds. Crucially, to achieve these ends, marriage must assume and reproduce the belief that the regulating authority is properly concerned with these ends. To alter actions by altering the most deeply held beliefs, marriage, like religion, assumes a relationship between individuals and community whereby the commands of the public authority are experienced as freedom-guiding, not freedom-limiting.

In this discussion, I use the terms "public" and "communal" and avoid the more appropriately Hegelian term—"the state." This allows us to isolate the centerpiece of Hegel's contribution to our investigation: a description of the social-psychological logic implicit in the widely held version of marriage, which distinguishes it, in form and function, from the various legal statuses (for example, civil union) and informal social institutions (for example, motherhood) to which it is often compared. He shows that marriage, like religion, is a formal, comprehensive social institution—which is to say that although it requires the express recognition of a public authority, it does not require the recognition of political authority in order to exist (or to flourish).

For Hegel, the *state* must serve as the ethical authority, for on his view, the national community is the community with which the individual must be reconciled. Both assumptions—that freedom requires this deep integration and that the national community is that with which individuals need to be reconciled—are, from a liberal perspective, problematic. If as liberals we reject Hegel's assumption of deep ideational homogeneity within and through the state, we may also reject Hegel's conclusion that the state can or should fill the role he assigns it vis-à-vis marriage. If marriage requires the affective recognition of some ethical authority and that authority has qualities that we do not—as an empirical or normative matter—associate with the liberal state, then some other authority must take the place of the state. We can do justice to the unique value of marriage and the role of external authority in generating that value without infringing on liberal commitments to freedom of thought and expression and to deep cultural diversity, which I explain in chapter 5, returning to Locke and Mill for insight.

This description of marriage as a formal, comprehensive social institution—more than a contract, instrumental legal institution, expressive resource, generic constitutive status, or informal social institution—is plausible, familiar, and useful. It fills out our picture of the meaning side of marriage, both in terms of *what* the extra value of marriage is (its unique capacity to integrate individuals to each other and to their community, from the inside out) and *how* it achieves this value (through the formal recognition and regulation of an ethical authority). This description helps make sense of the tensions in liberal theory and practice surveyed in earlier chapters even as it makes clear why the state should not be in the business of recognizing and regulating marriage as such.

The story that marriage has the capacity, in the right circumstances, to affect one's "moods and motivations"[39] and alter one's self-understanding in those predictable and deep ways is compelling. Something akin to this hyperconstitutive function of marriage has been part of the concept of marriage in the dominant traditions of Euro-American thought and practice at least since Locke's time. Something like this distinguishes it from both contract and civil union. This potential that marriage possesses and its institutional and ideational prerequisites are also the (buried) causes of liberal ambivalence toward state control of and reliance upon the institution. This is not to say that marriage always affects these ends, that it is the only means to these ends, or that everyone sees marriage in this vein. But that it might is plausible.

Crucially, this vision of marriage is also familiar. It is our vision, the view that dominates liberal traditions from the thought of Locke to the practice of American hippies in the 1960s. The presence of God in Locke's picture of marriage tells us, as does this account, that marriage is more than the contract or civil status he expressly describes. Marriage is a prepolitical institution in which the ethical authority par excellence—whatever it might be—plays a defining role. Locke may make marriage safer for the control of his limited, liberal state by functionalizing the institution. Yet as long as the state uses marriage as a vehicle for supporting its ends, it will also be engaged in a formal social institution.

This account of marriage both squares with and makes sense of tensions in Mill. Part of what makes his treatment of marriage so compelling is precisely his attention to the extralegal forces the legal status carries with it. While this description mirrors Mill's, it goes beyond it as well. As evident in his unconvincing response to Humboldt, Mill's attention to these forces wavers when he prescribes state action. When he holds that the state needs to recognize and regulate marriage to protect children and partners, he clearly worries about releasing from state control the extralegal powers of marriage. But he offers neither an explanation of what exactly would be lost nor a defense of the state's involvement in these goods. This account suggests that what would be lost in embracing Humboldt's proposal would be state involvement in the formation of social norms with regard to the most intimate areas of citizens' lives. This account also reveals the cost of this involvement: state enforcement of disputed ideas and norms. In *On Liberty*, Mill is deeply critical of such action. His silence, then, hides a deep tension.

This account of marriage helps make sense of what is going on (or what many assume is going on) when two people marry in front of a priest and members of their church community. They are dedicating themselves to a shared vision of their relationship, vis-à-vis each other and the recognizing community, and eliciting not only material support but emotional and ideational confirmation. The description also makes sense of secular marriage ceremonies. Consider a recent article in the *New York Times* "Styles" section, "Need a Minister? How about Your Brother?"[40] Reporter Rachel Lehmann-Haupt reviews the growing trend of couples turning to close friends and family to officiate at their weddings, facilitated by the easy, online availability of free, instant ordination (from organizations such as the Universal Life Church).[41] These couples lack any attachment to traditional (religious or legal) forms of authority but want a meaningful authority to confer their marital status nonetheless.[42] As one groom explained, "If you have no church, then you create your own authority figure. . . . You choose the person who has the most authority in your relationship."[43] The subjects of Lehmann-Haupt's article want the recognition of a public figure but do not have ready-made religious or legal authorities who fit that bill. Instead of abandoning formal, meaningful public recognition altogether, they draw an authoritative figure from their own community. A key advantage of this approach, many couples noted, was that it infused real meaning and significance into their ceremonies. In fact, many are driven to use alternative authority sources precisely because of the importance they place on the affective element of the public recognition of their union. As one prospective groom, Gavin Edwards, explained,

> It's not like we're anti-authority. . . . It's just that we didn't want a fake authority. I've been to weddings where it was clear that they had met the priest or whoever for the first time a week prior to the wedding. I'd seen that in Catholic, Jewish and the Ethical Society weddings. I wanted to avoid that. We chose our friend because he's a smart guy, has a lot of gravitas and he's a bit older then [sic] us. It wasn't like "la-la-la, you're married and here are some flowers." He treated the situation with the gravity that it deserved.[44]

Edwards and others like him assume that marriage is much more than a legal status or even an informal social institution. In terms of its purposes and methods, he suggests, marriage is a formal, comprehensive social institution.

This view is reflected in the claim that the state must retain exclusive control over the marital label to *protect* the institution. The logic of this account is precisely the logic that Francis Lieber shared with Hegel and that Chief Justice Morrison R. Waite took from Lieber and ensconced in

American law through his opinion in *Reynolds*. Justice Waite cites Lieber in defending his claim, "Upon [marriage] society may be said to be built, and out of its fruits spring social relations and social obligations and duties, with which government is necessarily required to deal."[45] Like Hegel, Lieber believed that marriage transforms the self-understanding, belief, and behavior of those party to it. Similarly, Lieber and Hegel shared the belief that the form and content of marriage, conveyed in the state's definition of the institution, affect the quality and character of these outcomes.[46] It helps us see why the state would want to control and use marriage. The public that defines, confers, and regulates marital status has the potential to wield unique power and influence over the generation of social norms and citizens' sense of self and of interdependence with the community. This helps explain both why the state would want to use marriage and not civil union and why the state wants to keep marriage to itself: to claim a monopoly on marriage is to hold the potential to generate a deep sense of obligation and interdependency between individuals and between individuals and the conferring community.

This account of marriage may explain what is special about marriage and thus why the state would want to control it. It may expose assumptions embedded in the views of many liberal theorists, jurists, and citizens. But it does not justify this arrangement. By treating marriage as a hyperconstitutive status and identifying the nature of the relationship required therein between individuals and the community, this account gives us reason to wonder whether the liberal state ought to serve as the primary public arbiter of such a status.

-5-

The Liberal Case for Disestablishing Marriage and Creating an Intimate Caregiving Union Status

Is there a good liberal case to be made for the establishment of marriage? In chapter 1, I argued that to answer this question we first needed to clear up the tensions and confusions that riddle the theory and practice of the state-marriage relationship in liberal traditions. This we did in the preceding four chapters. With the description of the logic of marriage as a formal, comprehensive social institution elaborated in chapter 4, we are now ready shift from a critical investigation of liberal discourse and practice, to normative argument.

In chapters 2 and 3, we extracted elements of a compelling liberal case for state involvement in intimate caregiving, but not in marriage per se. In search of such an argument, in chapter 4, we reconstructed the view of marriage that informs liberal traditions. We can now see why it is especially appropriate to speak of marriage as established. Just as the "establishment of religion" refers to the state's active involvement in defining, inculcating, and reproducing particular religious worldviews and institutional arrangements, so the "establishment of marriage" highlights the state's integral role in reproducing and relying on belief in a particular, comprehensive account and institutional form of intimate life and its tie to the community. The analogy suggests the answer to our central question: the establishment of marriage, like the establishment of religion, is deeply problematic. It violates basic liberal commitments to liberty and equality and threatens families and marriage itself. In the present chapter, I defend this claim and the most significant policy implications that I believe follow from it, first, that marriage be disestablished and second, that a regime of intimate caregiving union statuses be instantiated.

The existing relationship between marriage and the state threatens liberty and equality, fails to adequately protect and support intimate caregiving, and weakens marriage. There are two basic sets of problems with the establishment of marriage: The first concerns the role the state assumes when it wields final control over the public meaning and use of the marital label (the "authority problems"). The second stems from the use of marriage as the favored avenue through which the state protects and supports intimate caregiving (the "target problems").

The Authority Problem

Marriage not only "ratif[ies, but] fortifies relationships" by conveying constitutive or ethical recognition.[1] As we have just seen, marital status is more like a bar mitzvah or baptism than civil union—recognition intended to alter behavior by altering belief. The conferring authority must represent and defend a comprehensive story about the relationships (between the individuals in the couple and between the couple and the community) that it labels. The public performance of these accounts transforms by enacting, celebrating, and calling for public defense of the shared understandings they express. Like bar mitzvah or baptismal status, marital status is conferred with the aim of altering self-understandings, inculcating communal norms, and integrating individuals into the web of community. The ethical authority of a community of shared worldviews alters one's self-understanding. Defenders of the current regime fail to appreciate the serious and unnecessary costs—to marriage, families, liberty, and equality—of state involvement in and reliance on the reproduction of the constitutive purposes and effects of marriage. When government serves as the controlling public authority vis-à-vis marriage, it assumes the role of *ethical authority*, a role for which it neither is nor ought to be suited. The establishment of marriage casts the state in a role that it fills poorly and risks violating the type of neutrality necessary for the state to secure liberty and equality in a diverse polity such as ours. For all these reasons, the establishment of marriage weakens families.

Effective ethical authority rests on shared, comprehensive worldviews. Traditionally, liberals have treated the commands of the state as limiting action (not belief) for the narrow purposes of ensuring social order, protecting citizens from harm, and guaranteeing political fairness.[2] Generally, the state confers legal status for instrumental convenience, not to alter self-understanding in any deep and enduring way. The familiar idea behind the limited state is that freedom consists, in large part, in individuals being free from interference to live according to their own design.

In contrast, the role of the public authority in marriage is not merely incidental but rather integral to the potential of marriage. As the primary public authority in marriage, the state engages in a role whose basic purpose is to alter the self-understandings of those who assume and those who honor the label. The power of ethical authority rests on belief, shared by commander and commanded, in the ethical nature of their relationship. In the case of marital status, effective ethical authority assumes shared understandings of the nature of the relationships it labels (between the parties to marriage and between the couple and conferring community), of the purposes of the status, and, crucially, of the appropriateness of that authority's commands in matters of the most intimate nature. Recognition intended to alter self-understanding in this way we may call constitutive recognition, and the related status, constitutive status.[3]

Liberals reject the view of the state as ethical authority that such a position assumes. Since Locke defended the limits of the magistrate in *Two Treatises on Government* and *Letter Concerning Toleration*, liberals have rejected the notion that the state should function as an ethical authority in the sense assumed by the formal, comprehensive social institution of marriage.

As the comparison to religion makes clear, the state fails on two counts (beyond the equality issue discussed above) when it fills the role of primary controller of marriage. It fails liberty, and it fails marriage and the families it aims to protect. First, regarding liberty, the role of the public authority in marriage is not merely incidental; it is integral to the potential of marriage. As the primary public authority in marriage, the state engages in an institution whose basic purpose is to alter the self-understandings of those who assume and those who honor the label. In this controlling position, the state dominates the realm of belief and thus contravenes one of the most basic limits imposed in liberal theory to protect liberty, equality, religion, and the state itself.

Here, Locke's defense of toleration offers useful parallels. The distinct ends and means of church and state, he famously argues, demand their carefully guarded separation: to each its own realm. "The Boundaries on both sides [church and commonwealth] are fixed and immovable," he writes. "He jumbles Heaven and Earth together, the things most remote and opposite, who mixes these two Societies; which are in their Original, End, Business, and in every thing, perfectly distinct, and infinitely different from each other."[4] The sphere of the magistrate, that arena for which the state has the right to intervene and the appropriate—which is to say, effective—tools (law and the threat of force), is the physical world, and then only including those matters necessary to protect political liberty, equality, and stability. The commonwealth is constituted by men to advance and protect their "civil Interests." Thus, civil jurisdiction "reaches only to these Civil Concernments; and that all Civil Power, Right and Domination, is bounded and confined to the only care of promoting these things; and that it neither can nor ought in any manner to be extended to the Salvation of Souls."[5]

Locke makes clear the implications of this model when he considers the potentially confusing case of baptism and baby washing. What if the civil magistrate—or in our terms, the state—has good reasons (that is, related to public health) to encourage or require its citizens to engage in behavior (for example, baby washing) that is, coincidentally, also required by a church (for example, baptism)? The public good would seem to require state action while toleration might seem to counsel against it:

Let it be granted also, that if the Magistrate understand such washing to be profitable to the curing or preventing of any Disease that children are subject unto, and esteem the matter weighty enough to be taken care of by a Law, in that case he may order it to be done. But will any one therefore say, that a Magistrate has the same Right to ordain, by Law, that all Children shall be baptized by Priests, in the sacred Font, in order to the purification of their Souls?[6]

The magistrate cannot require citizens to baptize their children. He has neither the right nor the appropriate tools, authority, or, in light of the foregoing discussion of marriage, relevant relationship to his citizens to do so justly or effectively. Locke emphasizes the latter point. He writes that the salvation of men's souls cannot belong to the magistrate because "though the rigour of Laws and the force of Penalties were capable to convince and change Mens minds, yet would not that help at all to the Salvation of their Souls."[7] Yet if vulnerable individuals—infants, for instance—require regular washing for their survival, the magistrate has both the right and the appropriate sort of power (law and threat of force) to command their caregivers to wash them.

Locke's defense of toleration, at the heart of which lie these distinctions between action and thought, behavior and belief, and material and meaning matters, provided the conceptual seeds for the (largely) American liberal arguments for the nonestablishment of religion. Like Locke, early defenders of the separation of church and state emphasized not only the benefits to liberty and equality but to church and state.[8] For good historical and philosophical reasons, the role of the ethical authority is far more familiar to us liberals from the realm of religion than that of politics.

The liberal state is by design more distant and uninvolved with the beliefs of its citizens than the picture just sketched. Again, the familiar idea here is that freedom consists, in large part, of individuals being free from interference to live according to their own design. Marriage asks for and depends on much more from its regulating authority than what the liberal state can or should try to give.

In this role, the state also fails marriage and by extension all families who depend on its special powers to bolster their existence. The liberal state is ill-suited to serve as an ethical authority, so when it functions as the public authority of greatest significance vis-à-vis marriage, the state actually threatens marriage by undermining the force of its constitutive sway. Again, the example of bar mitzvah status is helpful. We would doubt both the effectiveness of the status and the justice of the action were the state to begin doling out bar mitzvah status. To effect its psychosocial transformation, the status must come from a community of shared religious belief and from Jewish religious leaders, from representatives of the community of belief that gives the status meaning. For the state to try to fill this role would rightly be seen as inappropriate—a violation of even the least restrictive variety of state neutrality—and, crucially, ineffective.

The Liberal Case for State Involvement in Intimate Caregiving

Marriage requires constitutive recognition from an ethical authority, yet the liberal democratic state cannot (and should not try to) effectively provide such recognition. The suggestion implicit in the comparison to religion—that there may be good reason for the state to withdraw from its pivotal role in controlling marital status—is compelling. For reasons I elaborate below, marriage, like the church in America, should not be established. Marriage must be disestablished. Crucially, this argument—that the state should get out of the business of defining and conferring marital status—implies little about the role the state should assume with respect to the material incidents typically associated with marriage. Leaving the definition and conferral of marital status to civil society is no different from leaving the control of baptismal status to civil society. In neither case do we assume that the state thereby withdraws from its role of protecting the vulnerable and promoting equality. On the contrary, as we began to see in chapters 2 and 3, there are very good reasons for the liberal state to recognize and protect intimate caregiving regardless of where it takes place. Though they speak the language of marriage, liberals emphasize material matters, especially those at stake in intimate care, where law or state action is concerned. Despite the language, they provide no real argument for state involvement in marriage per se. Looking past the marital veil, we discover a compelling liberal argument—stemming from a commitment to liberty, equality, and stability—for the state to play some role in supporting and protecting intimate care in all its guises.[9] Before turning to a full defense of the disestablishment of marriage, let us be clear about the force of these reasons.

Justice and prudence recommend that the state recognize and regulate unions within which intimate care is given and received: families, functional families, and networks of intimate care.[10] Contemporary scholars describe myriad relationships that fall into this category.[11] These include parents and children (biological and de facto); husband

and wife; long-term, cohabitating hetero- and homosexual lovers and partners; "lesbigay" units; nonsexually intimate adult units or groups;[12] adult siblings; adult children; and aging parents. In contemporary liberal democracies, intimate caregiving increasingly takes place in nonmarital settings: according to U.S. Census data from 2000, only 51.7 percent of households in the United States consisted of married couples, while cohabiting (nonmarital) households almost doubled between 1990 and 2000 to 5.5 million and nonfamily households (neither biologically nor legally related persons) increased 23 percent, more than double the rate of family households.[13]

The defining characteristics of intimate caregiving relationships include the following: first, they are largely and, to a degree ideally, unmonitored by outside parties. The day-to-day interactions in these relationships are not subject to direct regulation by public authorities. When this does happen, as with parents, especially single women, on welfare, we are rightly critical.[14] (Here, it is worth noting that intimate does not mean sexual, though intimate caregiving relationships may involve sexual intimacy.) The unmonitored or private character of these relationships allows their participants to give and receive care in accordance with their particular needs, desires, and—yes—power dynamics. So, for instance, privacy secures parents the freedom to raise their children as they wish or couples to engage in sexual practices of their liking.

Second, intimate caregiving relationships are characterized by deep (to the point of life-sustaining), diverse (material, emotional, physical, and spiritual), particular, and noncontractual "terms," ties, and motivations. While contract may serve as the background framework for some of these relationships—for many same-sex marriages today, for instance—they are not the guiding force of day-to-day interactions. So, for example, we expect partners in such relationships to give and take diverse and often incommensurable "goods" without guarantee of payback in kind. The noncontractual character distinguishes intimate caregiving from paid caregiving. While a nanny may be motivated by love for her charges, we would not be deeply troubled if she simply fulfilled the terms of her contract and were not motivated by love. Her relationship to her charges is, after all, not an intimate caregiving relationship in the sense that I have in mind.

Third, we see that strict, material reciprocation is not the primary mode of exchange in intimate caregiving relationships. While there is no doubt that financial exchange occurs and is quite often a source of power and grave injustices within relationships, both as a matter of fact and value, money is not the primary good of exchange in intimate caregiving relationships. Rather, these relationships involve exchange of diverse and often incommensurable goods and care—psychological, social, emotional, physical, spiritual, and, of course, financial and material. Furthermore, the exchange is only unpredictably, if ever, strictly reciprocal. Partly as a result, intimate care is best served by relatively stable, relatively long-term relationships to create time and space for a wide variety of exchange, and it usually though not always takes place in the context of relatively long-term, consistent cohabitation.

To be clear, the care of a psychotherapist, nanny, or home health assistant is not intimate in the sense I intend. The publicly monitored financial exchange that characterizes these relationships excludes them from my limited definition. Likewise, the counsel of a priest falls outside the realm of intimate care strictly defined because he or she is motivated and monitored by professional expectations. Conversely, the care provided by a single mother on welfare to her children, grandchildren, or stepchildren is intimate care, even though she receives money from the government and is, no doubt, overmonitored. The primary motivation of her labors is not the money or her contractual obligation to the state, the children, or the other parents of those children. Similarly, the care exchanged among a group of widows who have to some degree pooled their resources to live together and care for each other is what I call intimate care. The nature of "goods" exchanged, their flow and regulation, and even their motivation put such relationships in that category.[15]

This description of intimate caregiving is idealized, of course, though not unrealistic or undesirable. The examples of same-sex families and single parents on welfare show that the ideal of privacy is not always realized: until recently in the United States, states could and did outlaw sodomy, and they still do often intrude in egregious ways on the parenting practices of women on welfare.[16] At the same time, child abuse and marital rape demonstrate why total privacy is not worth pursing. Any ideal that can hide or justify marital rape is hardly worth defending. Feminists have shown how the notion that the state does not intervene in family life is a *dangerous* myth; not only does it hide inappropriate intrusions by the state, but it also explains nonintervention when it is justified (as in cases of marital rape).[17] They have also shown that contract, money, and raw power are constant factors in the ongoing bargaining between spouses.[18] Further, these scholars have shown how an ideal that ignores these facts can perpetuate grave injustice and harm (see chapter 3, for this discussion). No adequate account of intimate caregiving can ignore these insights, and mine does not. These insights lie at the heart of the argument of this book—that we must free public discourse and public law concerning intimate caregiving life from the distraction of *marriage*; only then will the true costs and benefits to individuals and society and the actual effects of this oft-hidden part of our communal life become clear and thus be addressed as justice and prudence recommend. Still, intimate care as defined here has many virtues. The aim of a liberal model of state involvement in intimate caregiving is to identify and protect those virtues without sacrificing liberty, equality, and stability.[19]

Intimate care is especially valuable because we could hardly be fully human without it. Plato's communist dystopia may be the Western canon's most famous reminder of this fact.[20] The thorough acquaintance and deep personal ties that characterize intimate relationships are especially suited to identifying and meeting the unique needs of others. Moreover, they allow for sustained, deep, and diverse connections that are essential to the healthy development of one's self and sense of justice.[21]

It is largely because they are intimate in the sense I have described that these relationships provide the kind of care that enables individuals to survive and flourish in mental, emotional, and physical ways that are uniquely valuable to individuals and to society. The privacy of intimate caregiving relationships is one of their key virtues; it facilitates relatively open exploration and development of diverse caring, partnering, and sexual practices. Two benefits flow from this fact. First, the experimentation that is enabled by this protection is a good not only as a reflection of liberty but also, as Mill argues in *On Liberty*, as a means to continual discovery of new and possibly better ways of living. It is, for instance, reasonable to hypothesize that the current flowering of diverse caregiving arrangements is a rational and ultimately positive response to social, economic, and technological changes. It is quite likely that one or many of these "alternative" arrangements is actually better suited than marriage to provide good care for the vulnerable in this new environment.[22]

Second, Drucilla Cornell has persuasively argued that the development of one's sexuate self is an essential aspect of overall human development and that a degree of protection from the leveling pressures of society is integral to this development.[23] The thorough, particular, and noncontractual ties and motivations of intimate care are especially conducive to the development of autonomy, interpersonal trust, and a strong sense of self.[24] Nonintrusion is also of great value to parenting. Scholars as diverse as Hannah Arendt, Jean Bethke Elshtain, Anna Marie Smith, and Linda McClain have argued that even (perhaps especially) democratic children need limits and reliable authority. When outside powers needlessly infringe on parental autonomy, this authority, and thus the quality of parenting, is weakened.[25] The privacy of intimate associational life benefits free, stable political life in another important way. Protected from outside interference, these relationships can serve as mediating institutions and sites of potential resistance to the totalizing tendencies of states.[26] In short, the privacy that characterizes intimate care relationships is good for individuals and for society. And still, for all its virtues, this privacy has many well-recorded vices. As numerous feminist scholars have shown, privacy often threatens equality, the vulnerable, and care itself.[27] Any adequate model of family policy must be sensitive to the virtues and vices of privacy.

In short, much if not most of the survival and nurturance care in our society takes place in intimate caregiving relationships, and this is good[28]: stable, intimate caregiving relationships are uniquely consonant with human diversity, dependency, and freedom. They are especially well suited to securing simultaneously the goods of deep interpersonal identification, trust, autonomy, responsibility, and physical well-being.

That care is essential and that intimate caregiving especially valuable to liberal democracies and their citizens are not quite enough to defend state involvement in intimate caregiving life, however. Friendships are essential and good, yet there is no good case for state recognition and regulation of these relationships. The difference is that intimate caregiving relationships are characterized by greater degrees of material and physical vulnerability, dependency, and risk than typical, nonintimate caregiving friendships are. As a result, they call for more substantial public involvement.

As we began to explore in chapter 3, giving care is risky. Providing care itself creates vulnerability. Caregivers must expend resources on care receivers that they might otherwise use to care for themselves. Caring for vulnerable people thus generates its own physical and material vulnerability.[29] Caregiving is risky in relationships between unequals (for example, parent and child) as well as those between equals. Though return of some sort may be expected, the unmonitored, unpredictable, and often incommensurable nature of caregiving means that it involves serious material, physical, and psychological risk, even among able-bodied, able-minded adults. The risk is especially significant when it takes place in intimate relationships because it is unpaid, unrecognized and undervalued, and not seen as producing "marketable" skills.[30]

As we saw in chapter 3, there are good liberal reasons for the state to be involved in ensuring against this risk: because intimate care generates systematic vulnerabilities and serious disincentives, any society that wishes this work to be done well and its benefits and burdens distributed justly (within and among families) must offer a degree of insurance against these risks. In a liberal framework, the state is the appropriate source of this insurance because it is the entity charged with the task and tools of protecting citizens from physical harm and securing a framework for the just distribution of the costs and benefits of political life. Furthermore, following Locke's implicit distinction between the actions in marriage and the institution itself, the state should provide this insurance for intimate care *wherever* it takes place. Both intimate care by a married couple for each other and intimate care by same-sex parents of their children are, in the senses outlined here, essential and risky. Nothing in the logic of the liberal case for state support of intimate care could justify the exclusion of the second family. If the individually and socially essential but risky labor of care is being exchanged, justice and necessity demand that the family be protected and supported.

Target Problems

With the liberal justification for state recognition and protection of intimate caregiving clear, we can now see how the government's use of marriage as the privileged model of family precipitates two undesirable consequences. First, as a matter of policy, an array of families with which the state *should* be concerned (but who are not defined by marriage) are unduly disadvantaged or excluded from its protective purview. Second, the establishment of marriage skews public discourse. The focus on marriage directs us toward the impossible task of defining marriage and distracts us from the matter of real import—how the state can foster the public-welfare goals associated with intimate caregiving and stave off the potential inequalities that occur within its folds.

If it is the case that the state has a key role to play in ensuring the labor of intimate care, then it follows from our commitments to equality, liberty, and stability that the state must recognize and support all unions within which intimate care is a central activity—families of all types. Thus, as it is currently crafted, state family policy fails families and violates liberty and equality because, very simply, it misses its mark. When marital status is the primary avenue for the flow of legal benefits, many families are left out or unduly disadvantaged.[31] In most jurisdictions, legal presumptions crafted to support the special commitments and risks of families—those concerning inheritance and adoption, for instance—are tied to marital status. In these instances, single-parent and same-sex families and groups of nonsexually intimate caregivers (siblings or postmarriage collectives, for example) are seriously disadvantaged. The state thus violates the principle of equality, of treating similarly situated citizens alike—in this case, intimate caregivers.

Moreover, because its protections serve some families more fully than others, this marriage-centered policy threatens equality among families and within families (between primary caregivers and others). Primary caregivers in families supported by the state have the insurance of predictable dissolution and inheritance policies to reduce the risk of their labor. This is not so for such caregivers in nonmarital families.

By missing the appropriate target of family policy, the establishment of marriage interferes with liberty. It violates what we might call freedom of marital expression when it prosecutes fundamentalist Mormons for using the label without prosecuting non-Mormons engaged in functionally similar relationships. More importantly, this arrangement violates liberty by limiting social insurance against the risks of intimate care; because intimate care done well and fairly depends on this insurance, its withholding threatens the freedom of intimate association. Think of same-sex adoptive parents whose joint parenthood is not presumed. Or unmarried long-term couples for whom joint home ownership is more expensive or riskier (if they opt not to pay lawyers to resolve the legal complications of their ownership). Both examples illustrate how people who wish to arrange their intimate caregiving lives outside the marital norm do not have the full range of freedom to do so under current policy.

The second target problem that arises from the establishment of marriage is that of skewed public discourse: the focus on marriage distracts us from the matter of real import and directs us toward the impossible task of defining marriage. The matter of real concern ought to be the costs, benefits, distribution, and needs of actual intimate caregiving arrangements. Does the paid labor force accommodate those who provide intimate care to children or elderly parents? When it does not, who "pays" and how? Women? Children? Underpaid public care providers? If the costs and benefits of care are to be acknowledged and justly distributed, they cannot remain hidden behind the veil of marriage. If the penalty for engaging in the essential labor of intimate care is to be lifted, its existence must be acknowledged in our public-policy debates. Government policy that focuses on marriage distracts us from these concerns.

At the same time, such policy directs our attention toward the impossible task of arriving at a widely shared, nontrivial definition of marriage. It is not surprising that citizens cannot agree on a substantive definition of marriage; integral ties to deeply divergent worldviews are what make marriage so important to people. These ties explain the difference between marital status and civil union. Even when marriage and civil union provide citizens with the same legal benefits (which they rarely do), they always *mean* different things.[32] The legal status of marriage draws on the reservoir of meaning attached to often-incommensurable visions of the institution that exists outside the law. And for this reason, we can hardly expect citizens to agree on a single definition of marriage.

As far as government policy is concerned, it is not problematic that citizens cannot agree upon a definition. The state need not take sides in *this* disagreement. What government must do is take sides on what counts as intimate care. This question will provoke controversy, of course. But compared to the controversy surrounding marriage, an open debate about what counts as a network of intimate care will be fairer and more fruitful. Such a debate will be more fruitful because the focus will be limited to questions about function and material concerns and restricted from larger questions about marriage. Discussions will thus be less infused with profoundly irreconcilable questions of religious beliefs or other comprehensive moral beliefs. By honing the focus of the debates, we increase our chances of finding common ground. To the extent that the discussion focuses on intimate caregiving of all sorts, it is also likely that the resulting policy will be fairer and more effective.

Many contemporary commentators, of course, reject the claim that marriage-centered family policy unduly disadvantages deserving families.[33] While they agree that the material well-being of families must be the driving concern of the state, they argue that, because of the proven benefits of marriage, public policy should channel people into its folds.[34] Government cannot be perfectly neutral with respect to all choices and must not be where the safety and well-being of children and caregivers are at issue. This pro-establishment camp argues that the benefits of crafting laws and regulations to discourage the formation of extramarital families far outweigh the costs. Some, whom we could call proestablishment conservatives, go a step further and argue that marriage should be reserved for hetero-monogamous couples.[35] While this position clearly violates liberal commitments, there is another version of the proestablishment position more fully committed to freedom of familial choice and equality within and among families. I call this the progressive-proestablishment position.[36] Defenders of this view hold that families of all forms deserve government support and that the problem with current policy is not its marriage-centricity, but rather its too-narrow definition of marriage. Same-sex marriage advocates and feminist scholars such as Mary Lyndon Shanley and Linda McClain argue that the legal status must be made available to couples who are "functionally equivalent" to heterosexual couples who may now assume the status.[37] Feminist proponents of this position pair their defense of expanding marriage with a serious concern for inequality within and among all types of intimate caregiving unions, and thus they advocate enhanced public support for all functional families, marital or not. Still, they expressly reject the call by a growing number of scholars for the abolition of marriage as a legal category.[38] The state should use marriage as a family policy tool because, they claim, it is especially well suited to providing intimate caregiving unions with the recognition, protection, and support they need.

The proestablishment progressives point to two features of marriage in defending the reformed establishment of marriage. Marriage, they argue, is especially well suited to the task of supporting intimate caregiving because it is a public *status*, not simply a contract. As a status, marriage provides a mechanism by which society (via the state) can ensure against the risks of intimate care without egregiously limiting choice within the union, undermining norms of unmonitored reciprocity, or bolstering preexisting inequalities.[39] Contract, in contrast, may facilitate individual choice, but as Carole Pateman and others argue, it merely reproduces existing power relations; given the pervasiveness of gender inequality and the inequalities inherent in intimate care, this is problematic.[40] Furthermore, contract requires that terms be delineated and held into the unforeseeable future. It thus threatens the norms of unpredictable and changing reciprocity that ideally characterize intimate relations. Contract is an inadequate tool for state protection of intimate caregiving unions, they argue, even when these unions only involve able adults (and not utter dependents).

Proestablishment progressives argue convincingly that status—a predetermined bundle of rights and responsibilities—can provide protection from egregious inequality by building equality protections into its terms, without violating privacy or undermining norms of noncontractual reciprocity. For example, in exchange for the benefit of being able to share material resources without taxation or monitoring, in most states in the U.S. couples agree to a presumed equitable division of material assets should they dissolve their union.[41] Status can also provide presumptive protection against state regulation of parenting practices without fully cordoning off the family from the demands of justice.[42] Status is thus the best mechanism for the state simultaneously to secure families against the risks of intimate care, support the norms of unmonitored reciprocity, and protect a significant degree of privacy. On this point, the proestablishment progressives are convincing.

Yet they do not, as they assume, make a case for marriage. All the virtues they attribute to marital status in terms of protecting intimate-care unions can be easily obtained with an instrumental status such as the proposed intimate caregiving union (ICGU) status. That marriage is a status does not justify its establishment.

The second feature that proestablishment progressives claim makes marriage an important focus of family policy is that marriage is not just any status, but a special status. Now we are back to the picture we sketched in chapter 4. In its groundbreaking decision, the Massachusetts Supreme Judicial Court wrote, "Civil marriage is at once a deeply personal commitment to another human being and a highly public celebration of the ideals of mutuality, companionship, intimacy, fidelity, and family."[43] Commentator Jonathan Rauch elaborates: "Marriage does much more than ratify relationships . . . [;] it fortifies relationships by embedding them in a dense web of social expectations."[44] Echoing Rauch, Shanley describes marriage as "a special bond and public status . . . a relationship that transcends the individual lives of the partners" in which the "public has a legitimate interest."[45]

As we saw in chapter 4, these claims about the potential of marriage are compelling. They do not, however, justify state control and use of the institution, as the proestablishment camp assumes. These commentators are right that marriage is more than an instrumental legal status. They go wrong, however, in their assumptions about the value and effects of government involvement in and use of this status and the extra value it carries.

The Case for Disestablishing
Marriage and Creating an ICGU Status

Marriage—like the church in America—should be disestablished. We can and should distinguish between instrumental and constitutive statuses. We can and should distinguish between marriage and the actions—intimate association and caregiving—often housed within its ideational folds. The state can achieve its legitimate public welfare goals—in this case, of protecting intimate association and caregiving—without defining and conferring marital status. In a diverse, liberal democratic polity such as the United States, freedom, equality, fairness, and *marriage itself* would be better served were marriage disestablished and an ICGU created.

Disestablishing marriage would mean that the state would withdraw from its current role in defining and controlling marriage; it would not confer marital status or use "marriage" as a category for dispersing benefits or assigning legal obligations. As a legal category, marriage would be abolished. As a cultural status, marriage would be left to voluntary associations, to religious and cultural entities that wield ethical authority more effectively and justly than does the state.

In place of marriage, we should create an ICGU status.[46] In many ways, an ICGU status would look like marital status today. It would afford legal recognition from which would flow various legal presumptions (lines of rights and responsibility), protection (that is, from certain types of intrusion), and material benefits (tax benefits). As with marital status now, an ICGU status would be defined, conferred, and, if necessary, dissolved by the state. Unlike marriage, however, ICGU would be expressly tailored to protecting intimate care in its various forms. So, for example, the status would reflect assumptions of longevity and resource sharing. Also, to protect the norms of unmonitored reciprocity and to protect caregivers, property would be divided upon dissolution in order to achieve substantive postdissolution equality. Crucially, ICGU status would be designed with instrumental rather than constitutive purposes in mind. Any special expressive significance attached to ICGU status would be incidental.

These reforms would address both the target and the authority problems of our current family policy and thus better realize our commitments to liberty, equality, and stability. They would shift the focus of public policy and discussion from marriage to intimate care. Exposing the real costs and benefits of caregiving would increase the chances that public support would be crafted effectively. For example, workplace policy would reflect the needs of all intimate caregivers by providing for universally available leave policies and flexible schedules. Policies would also be better targeted. Kinship presumptions, for example, would be as readily available to sexually intimate unions as to nonsexually intimate unions. Replacing marriage with a narrowly focused instrumental status as the primary means for supporting intimate caregiving would increase the chances that *all* actual caregivers would be served equally by government policy and treated equally before the law. Furthermore, the changes would benefit gender equality by exposing and more effectively addressing the realities of the derivative vulnerabilities and gender inequalities often created by current intimate caregiving arrangements.

An ICGU status would recognize and support *all actual* intimate caregiving relationships, many of which are ignored or denied under the current marital regime. Same-sex families and nonsexual caregiving partnerships are but two examples of units that would be able to avail themselves of this support under the proposed scheme.[47] ICGU has a second advantage for intimate care over the current system: it provides caregiving unions with all and only the benefits *they actually need* from the state. Replacing the hyperconstitutive status of marriage with the instrumental status of ICGU would address the target problem in public discourse: it would diminish the confusion and contradictions that plague current public discourse about why, how, and which types of intimate relationships deserve legal recognition and support. This change would shift the focus of public discussion from interminable disagreement about the definition of marriage to questions about the importance, nature and distribution of intimate care; likewise, it would expose the true costs and benefits of caregiving, thereby increasing the chances that they would be distributed fairly and that actual intimate caregiving unions would receive the protection and support they need. Defining caregiving would undoubtedly provoke controversy. But compared to that surrounding marriage, this controversy is likely to be much more fruitful from the perspectives of democracy and care. Arriving at a broadly shared definition of caregiving would be less challenging in part because it is more narrowly limited to questions about actions, not belief, which increases our chances of finding common ground. Discussions would thus be less infused with unspoken assumptions, hidden agendas, and profoundly irreconcilable questions of faith on the one hand

and on the other hand, expressly tuned to the basic material and physical costs and benefits of intimate care for individuals and society.

Disestablishing marriage and creating an ICGU status would address the target problem in policy: intimate caregiving unions do need recognition, but not, as many suggest, anything more than the recognition that comes with a legal label that provides a gateway for the legal and material protections and supports that help ensure that care is done well and its benefits and burdens distributed fairly. The ICGU status would be crafted with these aims in mind, and only these. So, for instance, the ICGU would provide legal presumptions such as next-of-kin privileges that encourage individuals to assume more, diverse, open-ended, and not strictly monitored responsibilities and risks than they might otherwise. To secure the privacy that we have seen is so essential to intimate care, IGCU status would provide a limited shield from government intrusion: so, for example, single parents on welfare who adopt the status—with its rights and responsibilities—would have an extra presumption against direct government control over their parenting decisions.

As with the current regime, the shield would not be as thick or broad as to protect harmful behavior. Spousal abuse, sex with minors, physical harm by parents would all justify state action, as they do or ought to do now. The trick of finding just the right amount of privacy is not peculiar to the ICGU status. The continual redrawing of privacy boundaries—for instance, with changing marital rape and privilege laws and with expanding protections for sexual practices—is evidence of this. The advantage of the ICGU as far as care (and, I shall argue, liberty and equality) is concerned is that it extends to *all* unions that actually deserve it, whatever the privacy that *any* intimate caregiving union deserves. As opposed to the marital regime, the protective net of which is at least too narrow (and possibly too wide), a targeted instrumental status is thus likely to serve intimate care quite well.

It is as a status in particular—that is, a bundle of rights and responsibilities—that the ICGU would benefit care. So with its protections and rights, the ICGU would also bring responsibilities and concrete legal obligations. It would not serve intimate care if it did not. So, for instance, parents (de facto or biological) would have a presumptive responsibility for the health and welfare of their charges. Failure to fulfill the basic standards on these counts could be grounds for state action. The issue here, of the right balance between parental authority and state intervention, is vast. The emerging scholarship and activism on children's rights are but two expressions of the complexity and importance of the issues. My brief comments here are not meant fully to engage them, but to outline in broad conceptual terms what an ICGU status would look like and why. The particulars of the status would need to respond to the insights of the literature surrounding these issues. ICGU status would obligate couples (or groups) to provisions designed to foster open-ended, unmonitored, and diverse exchange within the relationship, as in the case of equal property division postdissolution.[48]

Freedom of intimate association would also benefit under the proposed regime. By tying government benefits to the functions of intimate care, the ICGU would serve freedom of intimate association. So long as the adult parties to the unions consented to the status—with all of its rights and responsibilities—and their relationships met the basic criteria, the benefits of the ICGU would be theirs. To the extent that some types of intimate associations—caregiving ones, in particular—need outside support, the opening up (or narrowing down, depending on how you look at it) of the category would benefit freedom in this realm.

This claim raises two important questions. The first concerns children: should they not have a say in whether they are part of an ICGU? As my comment above suggests, I take this question seriously but shall not address it in depth here. For one, it is a question that would require another book altogether and is one on which many very good books and articles have been written.[49] For another, the issues are roughly the same under our current regime. Why should a child be forced to be part of a marital family? Or step- or foster-family? The answers would differ little were the status marriage or an ICGU.

The second question concerns adults, specifically adults in relationships with adults only. Does not liberty demand that their relationships be regulated by contract? Martha Fineman advocates this position. For many of the reasons outlined above, but especially those concerning care and equality, she argues that family policy should be built around the caretaker-dependent dyad and not the married couple: "I am not concerned with the nature of the relationship between sexually affiliated adults—the husband-wife dyad. I have argued that such a focus distorts policy discussions, masking important issues concerning dependency and caretaking for those who are in need, including children and many of the elderly, the ill, and the disabled." For caretaker-dependent relationships, Fineman expressly rejects the contractual model and thus resists the "contract-plus" label.[50] Yet she advocates the use of contract to regulate relations between adult sexual affiliates. "Marriage" distracts and should be abolished as a legal category, she argues. Instead, "interactions of female and male sexual affiliates would be governed by the same rules that regulate other interactions in our society—specifically those of contract and property, as well as tort and criminal law."[51] It is this element of Fineman's approach with which I disagree. Though it may not be her central concern, it is useful given my focus to label hers the "contract-plus" option.

Fineman's argument for bringing dependency and care to the fore is entirely persuasive. I draw from and follow much of her argument. Yet in her important and persuasive effort to shift public discourse and policy away from the married couple, she leaves a key category of intimate caregiving relationships dangerously unprotected and unsupported. As I make clear above, adult-adult intimate caregiving relationships also involve essential and risky care labor. They too, then, need the special recognition and protection that only a status can offer. In short, liberty on its own does recommend that adult-to-adult relations be governed by contract, but liberty is far from our only value. Equality, protection from harm, and a rough version of the public good all recommend not only that the state offer the option that these relationships be regulated by status, but even that it limit the allowable terms of such contracts when chosen.

Freedom of association would benefit in another way. As we saw in chapter 2, marriage has long served to justify protection of this freedom in the American constitutional tradition.[52] Doing away with the marital category would be one crucial step in dislodging marriage from its seat as the reigning proxy for relationships that need and deserve such protection. The move would help highlight the fact that all human beings, married or not, heterosexual, homosexual, single, paired, sexual, or celibate, need a space within which to imagine and enact their social intimate lives. Furthermore, just as the nonestablishment of religion ensures that a citizen's right to vote cannot depend on her religious affiliation, so too the disestablishment of marriage would guarantee that government-provided benefits for intimate caregiving would not hinge on an individual's public acceptance of a particular vision of marriage. Disentangling marriage from government support of intimate caregiving would therefore solve the target problem of current policy.

Disestablishing marriage and creating an ICGU would also address the authority problem. Government authority, unique though circumscribed as it is, would concern itself with the basic physical and material security of its citizens, not with their beliefs. On the most basic level, releasing "marriage" from the hands of government would protect a unique kind of expression. Unlike under the current regime where citizens can be prosecuted for unsanctioned use of the marital title—as was polygamist Tom Green[53]—under the proposed regime, citizens who wished to call themselves married could do so without fear of state punishment. As with bar mitzvah status, nongovernmental authorities would confer the label. While it would carry no legal weight, marriage would still carry its constitutive potential. Call this the freedom of marital expression.

Some might think this a trivial freedom. But the arguments of the preceding chapters, the movements for and against same-sex marriage, and the fact that increasing numbers of people are marrying outside the scope of the law (polygamous, heterosexual, and same-sex unions) suggest just the opposite. To individuals and the communities that recognize these unions, "marriage" is a label that carries weighty significance even when the state is not its source. In the legal setting, the difference between marriage and civil union shows precisely that "the 'm' word" does matter:

as a historical fact, it carries social significance that legal recognition can never create or eradicate on its own. So, the freedom of marital expression is far from trivial.

Individuals might, of course, use this freedom to trivial ends, and one can easily imagine many ways that individuals could do so. But as Britney Spears in Las Vegas and "Who Wants to Marry a Millionaire?" remind us, the current regime suffers no shortage of people who trivialize their freedom.[54] Releasing the label of "marriage" from control by the state is not likely to make matters worse. Moreover, and perhaps more importantly, the fact that many individuals use the freedom of expression traditionally conceived for trivial ends is not thought to undercut the necessity of protecting that freedom. To call oneself married is, at its most powerful, to say something profound about one's connection to another individual and to a particular community. Protecting the opportunity to exercise this form of expression is thus of fundamental importance.

Ah, but this is a trivializing freedom, one might worry. Surely leaving the conjugal appellation to the whims of individual choice would effectively undercut its constitutive and transformative power for *all* by undermining its necessarily communal foundation!

While understandable in a context in which "public" and "state" are often conflated, this concern is misguided. Far from trivializing the public conferral and acceptance of marital status, protecting the freedom of marital expression would more likely elevate and thus strengthen the significance of this social exchange in at least two ways. First, if the extra value of marital status stems from its association with ethical authority, then *state* control is not essential to its realization. Just the opposite: if we follow the comparison to religion, history would seem to be on our side in the prediction that the unique expressive value of marriage would increase were the state to relinquish control over the institution. Like its religious kin, ethical authority in marriage depends on being chosen in one sense but also *not* chosen, in the sense that it just *is* experienced as ethical authority by its adherents. The constitutive potential of marital status is thus more likely to be realized or felt when the conferring authority is chosen/not chosen in this sense. Such an authority might, for some people, be a religious leader. For others, an ethical authority might be the head of a cultural group or the esteemed representative of one's family. The key to effective ethical authority in marriage is that the conferrer and recipients share the understanding that the conferrer possesses the authority to bestow the resulting responsibility that their shared vision of marriage entails. Nonstate entities—associations of civil society—represent just such potential authorities. By releasing "marriage" from state control into the arms of these entities, the nonestablishment of marriage places control of this constitutive status in the hands of those best suited to wield it effectively. Therefore, marriage is likely to benefit.

Second, under the proposed regime, acquiring marital status would be the ticket to the ethical recognition of a community of shared understandings and not to a vast array of legal and material benefits. Changing the benefits would change the motivations for seeking the status. As many same-sex couples do already, couples would acquire marital status when they wanted meaningful recognition from a community that held ethical sway in their lives.[55] Moreover, shifting control of marital status to voluntary groups in civil society would increase the likelihood that marital status would be acquired in the context of a community of shared understandings about marriage. This improved fit between the couple's understanding of marriage and that of the conferring community could also bolster the transformative force of marital status. By shifting control of marriage to cultural authorities and their diverse and, admittedly, not always liberal accounts of marriage, the proposed regime would benefit marriage by invigorating the constitutive force of the status.

Disestablishment of marriage would strengthen the power of ethical authorities and their diverse versions of marriage. In the face of the state's definition and conferral of marital status, other religious, cultural, ethnic, and familial authorities, which now technically share responsibility for this task, find their effectiveness compromised. To borrow an insight from the field of economics, the state has the tendency to "crowd out" other sources of authority.[56] From markets to social welfare to education, when the state moves in, its presence is overwhelming, though it technically shares control with other authorities. Because of the state's unique control of material goods, legal force, and legitimized power of coercion, people tend to view the state as the most important authority in any arena it enters, even if upon careful consideration they might not attribute this prominence to the state in all matters within that arena. It is reasonable to assume that this is the case with marriage: almost unconsciously, people view the state as the public authority of most immediate, if not sole, consequence in marriage. Communal authorities that might be able more easily to call upon the shared understandings necessary for effective constitutive recognition find themselves crowded out by the expansive presence of the state.[57]

The state's withdrawal from the position of the primary arbiter of marital status would open an authority vacuum. Into this void would enter the alternative sources of constitutive recognition that currently compete with the state—and now without the unmatchable competition of the state. This move would expand opportunities for diverse cultural groups to fill a uniquely significant role of public authority. By reclaiming this special role, cultural groups— everything from religious organizations to secular, social, and political community groups to tight-knit families and friends—would be infused with new significance. Given more space to function as the controlling authority vis-à-vis marriage, such public groups would gain effectiveness, recognized by the public at large as more authoritative. Call this the positive-feedback effect.

Just as disestablishing marriage would benefit diverse ethical authorities, it would also energize their different accounts of marriage. The content of nonlegal accounts of marriage suffers when marital status is conferred by the state. Under the current regime, the state's definition of marriage has a powerful influence on the way that people think of marriage, if only because of its unique association with material and legal benefits. The expansive presence of this definition undermines the unique value of the status by thinning the diverse accounts that "marriage" implies and pressuring them into insignificance. In the spirit of protecting equality, individual freedom, and cultural and religious pluralism, the state aims to convey an account that is accepted by all or most of its citizens. Where marriage is explicitly defined, as in the Defense of Marriage Act, the definition is notably thin and reflects the state's wariness about imposing a particular definition of marriage: "the word 'marriage' means only a legal union between one man and one woman as husband and wife, and the word 'spouse' refers only to a person of the opposite sex who is a husband or a wife."[58] This thin, wary definition is as it should be, as far as the liberal state is concerned.

As far as marriage is concerned, however, this definition is problematic. When the account that dominates is narrow, uniform, and based on the thinnest of shared understandings, it weakens the unique social force of marital status. The unique transformative potential of marital status depends in part on a relatively comprehensive account of the new relationships (between the parties to marriage and between the couple and the community). The institution of marriage, therefore, suffers under state control. By extension, removing the state's definition of marriage from the range of available options would create a "definitional vacuum" into which diverse cultural groups would carry their unique and complex definitions of marriage. Now unimpeded by the stifling and weighted competition of the state's definition, other definitions would gain social prominence, in turn enhancing their expressive value. By invigorating cultural authorities and by giving room to their diverse and complex accounts of marriage, the proposed regime would benefit marriage by invigorating the constitutive force of the status.

For those skeptical about the claim that informal, secular groups will produce ethical authorities capable of conferring effective constitutive recognition, recall the young couples in the *New York Times* article cited in chapter 4: these nonreligious couples are finding their own ethical authorities outside both church and state. By infusing the choice to assume marital status with greater intentionality and by invigorating cultural authorities and their diverse accounts of marriage, the abolition of the legal status of marriage would bolster the very forces that are essential to the unique constitutive value of marital status. If I am right about what makes marriage special and the properly limited capacity of the liberal state to help foster this unique value by defining and conferring the status, then liberty and marriage would likely be better off were the state to withdraw from this role.

My proposal is likely to elicit numerous concerns. Here, I address three. The first concerns gender equality: if marriage is left to associations of civil society, do we not run the risk of pushing the inequality and oppression often shrouded behind the conjugal veil further from public scrutiny? For instance, would not disestablishing marriage effectively allow polygamy and, therefore, promote gender inequality? This worry invites three responses: first, if marriage were disestablished, some groups would openly sanction polygamous marriage, and gender inequality would undoubtedly flourish in many of these unions. These groups might assume ICGU status. They would, therefore, gain support and protection from the state. Crucially, however, they would receive support by virtue of their willingness to enter into the civil status, with its protections and responsibilities for caregiving activities. In this sense, my proposal promotes gender inequality no more than do current regimes that permit but do not ostensibly promote traditional (gendered) marriage.[59] Second, gender equality would benefit under the proposed regime because the increased recognition of and support for caregiving would ensure that even women who opted for traditional gendered marriages would be less vulnerable as a result of the gendered division of power and labor within their families. Public policies would be crafted to protect all intimate caregivers; those who opt to care full-time might, for instance, receive financial support from the government. Less radically, unpaid labor would be factored into postdivorce settlements. Still, the critic might say, the proposal promises to increase the power of potentially illiberal communities and thus increase their sway over the way people *think* and behave, and this is no small power. To this, I offer a third response: we must balance liberty, equality, and stability. Even with this very real danger, I believe that the proposed model does a better job balancing these commitments. It increases liberty by limiting the objects and intent of state action without relinquishing influence over the most significant sources of inequality and instability (especially the material and physical risks assumed by primary caregivers).

The second objection contends that mine is a rather incoherent "anything-goes" policy. This worry is misplaced. Both marriage and ICGU status reflect value judgments. In defining and conferring either status, the state is acting in a way that reflects particular political commitments. There are compelling liberal reasons for the state to recognize, protect, and support intimate caregiving. The case against state control of marriage is not that it reflects a substantive commitment, but rather that it entangles the state in an institution whose primary purpose is to alter self-understanding in ways that go beyond what is necessary to the legitimate public-welfare concerns of the state. I agree with these critics that "marriage" matters: it carries a unique value beyond the material and legal benefits that attach to it, even beyond the generic expressive goods that come with any legally privileged position. To ignore this extra value is naïve and detrimental to marriage, equality, liberty, and fairness. But marriage is not the only or even the best means by which stable caregiving relationships can be understood and protected. For the sake of the potential benefits to those who are moved by marriage, it is an institution that should be afforded public support and protection. From civil society, marriage can receive its constitutive recognition. From the state, marriage and all other caregiving relationships can and should receive instrumental support.

The final concern I call the single-person's worry. The objection runs something like this: if the liberal democratic state is concerned with protecting the vulnerable, treating citizens equally before the law, and respecting individual choice, this policy fails on every count. Notice, to start with, that ICGU status benefits some people—nonsingles—at the expense (via taxes) of others—singles. Such inequality must be justified by compelling state interest. If the underlying justification for an ICGU status is protecting the vulnerable, the justification fails. After all, single people are the most vulnerable, for it is they who have no reliable, legally recognized, and protected source of intimate caregiving. Far from asking single people to support the privileged lives of others (that is, their intimate care), the state should be doling out benefits to single people—stipends for dating services, laundry service, and take-out meals. Supporting single people in this manner would protect the right to choose how to order one's intimate caregiving life.

This concern is compelling. Single people are uniquely vulnerable. And being single is not always a choice. (The popularity of online matchmaking services such as Match.com would suggest just the opposite.) The demands of fairness and care do have force here. They do not, however, undermine the case for establishing an ICGU. For one, ICGU status is crafted to protect those who engage in the essential but risky business of caregiving. To the extent that everyone, even single people, needs care and generally prefers intimate care, the state ought to protect it.[60] It is important to note that even single people benefit from the intimate care they do not themselves receive. To the extent that this care supports the survival and nurturance of fellow citizens, and hence society as a whole, single people benefit from that care. Care, after all, is what produces our fellow citizens, students in our classrooms, workers in our stores and factories and fields, and business people, politicians, and bums. Nobody, not even a single person, fails to benefit in very concrete ways from the unpaid labor that is given and received in the risky realm of intimate caregiving relationships. In addition, I take the risks of singledom to be among the justifications for a more robust system of social services—health and child care primary among them. I am not prepared to say, however, that this safety net should be made so robust as to take away the special burdens altogether. Such a scheme would have two major disadvantages. It would amount to a system of total and direct provision of intimate care by the state. As I argue above, efficiency, justice, and human connection would all suffer under such a regime. Such a scheme would discourage the risky but uniquely valuable behavior of intimate caregiving that, ideally and at least often, takes place in families and other contemporary caregiving units.

The case for nonestablishment of religion was not a case for the state to get out of the business of education, social services, public health, or criminalizing that took place in the church. The magistrate can still command citizens to wash their children if public health requires. Leaving the definition and conferral of marital status to civil society is no different from leaving the control of baptismal status to civil society. In neither case do we assume that the state thereby withdraws from its role in protecting the vulnerable, guarding equality, and securing what Locke calls "the public good"—the material preconditions for its own reproduction.[61] What we *do* assume is that the best way to balance liberty, equality, and stability in a diverse society is for the state to be concerned primarily with regulating action and material concerns, not expression or thought—and then only to the extent necessary to protect other citizens from harm and to guarantee the basic material preconditions for free and fair political life. Any argument that ignores the material concerns treated through marriage would be inadequate indeed. To deliver its promise of equality among and within intimate associations, freedom of intimate association, and protection from harm for all vulnerable individuals regardless of the public label of the relationships they inhabit, the liberal case for disestablishing marriage must include an argument for the creation of an ICGU status.

Reconsidering the Public/Private Divide

*T*he union of marriage and the liberal state is an uneasy one—and for good reason, as we have seen. Our commitments to liberty, equality, and stability recommend against it. Is the policy of disestablishing marriage radical? In some sense, yes. It would clearly be an enormous break with past practice. But the policy squares with many of our most basic political values; it is the right, if surprising, thing to do.

We now turn to our principles and to liberal political theory more generally. The lessons here extend beyond contemporary family law and policy. At the conclusion of our investigation, we came face to face with questions about how a society such as ours—one that celebrates real equality, individual freedom, and the deep diversity that flows from both—should manage its common costs. How do we balance liberty, equality, and stability in the face of the facts of human interdependence and deep diversity? Liberal political theory offers answers to these questions. And while this study focuses specifically on the relationship between marriage and the state, the book also serves as a critical look at answers to those broader questions and a source of ideas for crafting more compelling solutions.

Marriage/state relations serve as a direct road into the heart of liberal political theory, to that area where public and private meet, overlap, and collide. Engaging in the on-going task of evaluating and renegotiating this divide is one important contribution of this book. So although marriage is the immediate focus, the conceptual considerations here speak to broader concerns within liberal political theory. As liberals, multiculturalists, and feminists have shown, questions about the public/private divide are at the heart of the dilemmas raised by the increased cultural, ethnic, and religious diversity of most liberal democratic polities.[1] From headscarves to voting rights, religious law in liberal democracies, cultural-group rights, and debates about same-sex parents and adoption policy, the present considerations help craft a liberal vision of political life that does best by stability, individual freedom, group autonomy, and real equality between and within ethnic, racial, cultural, and familial groups.

Such a vision must be sensitive to the nature of today's global political economy—to the expanding power of multinational corporations and the changing position of the nation-state. It must account for the increasing cultural and ethnic diversity within porous national borders and for the growing economic and environmental inequalities. More narrowly, this book reminds us that a compelling account of how we should live together should address three challenges. First, it must balance the goal of individual autonomy with the fact of human interdependence. On this count, attention to the oft-hidden costs of care and gender inequality is paramount. Given the nature of intimate care, as we have seen, neither freedom nor equality nor stability can be secured by a state that merely protects individuals from external impediment. The state must recognize and regulate intimate caregiving units to insure against the inherent risks of care, but it must do so in ways that neither undermine their norms of reciprocity nor exacerbate existing inequalities. Second, such a theory must take seriously the demands both of group autonomy—familial, cultural, religious, national, and moral—*and* individual freedom and equality. In a world where porous national borders produce unprecedented religious, cultural, ethnic, and moral diversity, this challenge is especially pressing.[2] Third, a viable and compelling vision of the good political life must manage these balancing acts as a means to and in the context of attending to the need for basic political, economic, and social stability.

This book demonstrates the enduring utility of the public/private divide as a conceptual tool for negotiating these challenges and crafting such a theory. "Public" and "private" are not stable, self-evident, or uncontested terms. Broadly, "public" refers to those areas and issues of communal life with respect to which the state legitimately acts, where shared standards of political cooperation rule, and where universal laws govern.[3] "Private" signals areas and issues where direct state action is inappropriate, which is to say illegitimate, oppressive, and ineffective. As Judith Shklar writes,

> The limits of coercion begin, though they do not end, with a prohibition upon invading a private realm, which originally was a matter of religious faith, but which has changed and will go on changing as objects of belief and the sense of privacy alter in response to the technological

and military character of governments and the productive relationships that prevail.[4]

Thinkers from across the political spectrum have criticized liberalism's reliance on this divide.[5] To many, the conclusion that we should revive the public/private distinction will sound downright archaic; to others, naïve, deeply mistaken, and dangerous. Some, including John Stuart Mill, Jean Bethke Elshtain, Susan Moller Okin, and Raymond Geuss, argue convincingly that the line is an illusion, that it hardly describes anything about real life. The illusion, they argue, is dangerous because it helps obscure or hide injustice and oppression.[6] The myth of the public/private divide, they show, exacerbates inequality: unequal power in private quickly translates into unequal power in public, and vice versa. Many critics note that the distinction between public and private spheres has also been used to justify oppression: what a man does to his wife in the privacy of his home, the argument goes, is none of the magistrate's business. And the private becomes a venue for the rise of oppression and inequality.

The present study has roots in these critiques of the public/private divide. For any student of political theory in an American university in the 1990s, liberalism was a central focus. Of the many critiques of the dominant political theory, feminists offered one of the most compelling. Liberalism promised freedom and equality *for all*, yet few classical liberal thinkers or the political regimes they influenced included women as equals. Exposing the inconsistency and identifying the solution were relatively straightforward tasks. Feminists went further, explaining why formal equality was not enough. Built into the liberal tradition as a conceptual framework, empirical claim, and normative standard was the public/private divide, which undermined the possibility of real freedom and equality between the sexes. As both prescription and description, the distinction between public and private life helps to sustain and exacerbate inequalities, all under the guise of formal equality, and thus undermines liberalism's professed promise of freedom and equality for all.[7] The power of this critique is undeniable. So why return to the public/private divide?

For feminists, as we have seen, the paradigmatic instance of the problems with this liberal attachment is marriage—not the state's involvement in the institution but the inequality that its present arrangement can manifest. Liberal reliance on a distinction between public and private matters and between political and nonpolitical matters obscures and exacerbates the facts of inequality within marriage and their influence on power outside it. Feminists showed that real equality and liberty require the division between public and private life to be recognized for what it is—a myth—and its prescriptive rule to be questioned.[8] Inequalities within gendered marriage and family, that is, "the private," affect power in the public sphere. As we saw in chapter 3, theorists like Mill and Okin persuasively argued that political principles of consent and equality must apply to relations within marriage and the family.

These arguments are compelling. And on one reading, at least, they raise doubts about liberalism as a whole. The promise of liberalism rests on distinguishing public from private life. In public, citizens must conform to universal laws; like individuals must face like treatment before a known standard and impartial judge. In private, difference may reign. From John Locke to John Rawls, this has been the gist of the liberal solution to the problem of how deeply diverse people can live together in relatively just stability.

Very compelling feminist criticism of the divide thus appears to threaten the whole liberal house. But while some "radical" feminists such as Zillah Eisenstein appreciated the depth of the challenge, most liberal feminists turned their attention elsewhere. The challenge, however, is potentially fundamental. Neither liberals nor feminists can afford to avoid it.

And to face the challenge head on, one need turn no further than back to marriage. The very fact that it straddles the public/private divide makes the institution an ideal site for thinking through the question of how, if at all, liberal political theory can be remade to deliver on its promise of offering a rough template for a just and secure political life. And it shows that liberalism can make sense of the gray zone that separates private from public.

Collapsing the distinction between public and private and subjecting family life to the full, unmediated strictures of political justice, especially regulation and enforcement by the state, would endanger the very autonomy that feminists rightly celebrate.[9] Limits on state action serve freedom of thought and discussion, and this is good for both the individual and society. Such limits also conduce to what Mill calls "experiments in living." Theorists of multiculturalism have shown that limiting the reach of the state can, in crucial instances, bolster cultural cohesion and independence. The deep diversity that flourishes as a result, while potentially threatening to stability—itself a reason to limit certain practices—can be good for individuals, groups, and society as a whole. Finally, privacy from government intrusion can be essential to fostering familial/parental authority *and* norms of noncontractual give and take that ideally characterize at least a part of intimate caregiving life. All these are goods that feminists rightly defend.

As Shklar crucially points out, "It is a shifting line, but not an erasable one, and it leaves liberals free to espouse a very large range of philosophical and religious beliefs." The question then becomes where to draw the line. In one sense, the answer to this question is simply, "somewhere." As Shklar writes, "The important point for liberalism is not so much where the line is drawn, as that it be drawn, and that it must under no circumstances be ignored or forgotten."[10] Furthermore, as our examination of marriage shows, we must not think that, once drawn, the line must remain "there" forever—or even that it is a perfectly identifiable line. On the contrary, the line should shift with changing social and political norms. And because of its history of and ability to contribute to injustice, the location and uses of the conceptual tool must be the objects of continual critical scrutiny. Feminist and other critiques of the public/private divide *are* compelling. Caution *is* warranted when invoking the public/private divide. But caution does not mean abandoning the tool altogether. We can and should sketch a provisional line through public and private matters.

We do well to draw on the framework given to us by classical liberals such as Locke and Mill. State action should never intrude on the realm of thought. Belief and conscience should be left unfettered by intentional government massaging. Does this mean that government policies do not influence the way citizens think? Of course not. But it does mean that government policies ought not be crafted to alter the self-understandings of citizens through and through. On this principle, the second Bush administration's recent campaign to promote marriage as a welfare policy is problematic.[11] Aim at the action, not at the comprehensive moral veil in which the actions are diversely cloaked. We might also question, for instance, the recent ruling by a French court to deny citizenship to a devout Muslim because wearing her headscarf indicated insufficient integration into secular norms.[12] As long as she acts according to the public laws, what she appears to believe about them or the social norms they do not regulate ought to be irrelevant to the state. Where action is at issue, it should be allowed as long as the action does not harm another person. I should be allowed to grow corn on my hillside, unless, of course, my doing so harms others. Then it may be subject to common regulation. (There will be deep disagreements about whether actions harm others, of course, but this does not obviate the utility of the principle as a guide.)

In deeply diverse polities, limiting the reach of the organized state to matters of material concern, action, and behavior and restricting it from thought and belief are the best of the range of available and imperfect strategies. *And the imperfection must be center stage.* Belief and behavior are not conceptually, historically, or empirically totally distinguishable. We therefore need to notice and be vigilant toward the potential for the use of the distinction to violate, oppress, and exclude.

In conclusion, let us recall Aristotle's warning about method: aim for precision appropriate to the subject.[13] In the present case, a vision of the good political life and the means to achieving it are subjects rife with unknowns and hence opportunities for *judgment*.[14] A good theory is a rough guide, not a mathematical formula. A critical instinct—concerning the ends, the means, and the theory itself—must be cultivated and kept on high alert. In that spirit, consider this a temporary revision, subject to ongoing reform in the face of changing material, ideological, social, economic, and political norms and forms. The line between public and private is never perfectly clear, stable, or distinct. It is always only a conceptual divide, one that can help or hinder our efforts to envision and enliven a just, stable, and free political coexistence.[15] Like Shklar, I do not claim that the distinction is natural or unchanging, only that it is necessary to secure freedom, equality, and stability in times of increasing diversity.

This book contributes to this project of redrawing the line between public and private life, thereby bringing us closer to achieving liberalism's promise of liberty and equality in the face of deep diversity. Facing up to the troublesome character of this relationship draws us to the very heart of the liberal approach of governing free and diverse citizens. The liberal approach is both viable and valuable, but the current relationship between marriage and the state does not square with that approach. Understanding and resolving these conflicts are necessary if liberalism's promise of balancing freedom, equality, and stability in diverse polities is to come anywhere close to being fulfilled. By contributing to the essential and ongoing project of scrutinizing and redrawing the proper limits and reaches of state action, this work helps liberalism address these challenges. It helps craft a liberal theory that provides a viable, compelling guide for negotiating freedom with equality, independence with interdependence, and deep cultural, religious, and moral diversity with the unity needed to coexist in peace.

Notes

CHAPTER ONE
TOWARD A LIBERAL THEORY OF MARRIAGE AND THE STATE

1. Varney, "Gay-Rights Pioneers Wed."
2. Waldman, "Rick Warren's Controversial Comments."
3. Varney, "Gay-Rights Pioneers Wed."
4. Although I refer primarily to the United States, this description applies to other liberal democracies. See, for example, Belgium, France, and Great Britain in Boele-Woelki and Fuchs, *Legal Recognition of Same-Sex Couples*, and Hamilton and Perry, *Family Law in Europe*. (I thank Matthew Guarnieri for research assistance on this topic.) I borrow the term "established" from Nancy Cott in her very important work *Public Vows: A History of Marriage and the Nation*. Lisa Duggan also uses the term in her work. The definition here draws on Cott's but is my own. Note that this is different from "institutionalize"—as in "deinstitutionalized"—a term used by many writers today to describe a related but distinct phenomenon. The difference is that "established" refers to the role of the state in marriage. Institutionalization includes and goes beyond the state's engagement with marriage; it refers to the general state of marriage as a social institution. See Blankenhorn, *The Future of Marriage*. While neither synonymous with nor a direct effect of the establishment of religion, the establishment of marriage is historically correlated with and conceptually akin to the former. I use the term to refer to a historically specific arrangement where the state actively controls, privileges, and utilizes a particular account of marriage to regulate the intimate and caregiving lives of its citizens.

5. Marriage is established despite the fact that citizens hold deeply divergent views of what marriage *is* and how intimate life ought to be arranged, as evinced by debates concerning same-sex marriage, high divorce rates, and divergent views on infidelity, polygamy, and the proper roles of husband and wife. The flourishing diversity of family forms highlights the lack of consensus—in theory and practice—regarding intimate caregiving life (Stacey, "Toward Equal Regard for Marriages").

By some accounts, the establishment of marriage is weakening. In the United States, Cott identifies an uneven but steady trend toward the state's relinquishing control over the conjugal union (*Public Vows*, 212). Similar trends are evident across Europe. To be sure, contrary developments are also evident, among them federal and state laws that define marriage as a heterosexual union and the advent of covenant marriage (*Public Vows*, 213).

6. Peters and Kamp Dush, *Marriage and Family*; Metz, "Liberal Case for Disestablishing Marriage"; Fineman, *Neutered Mother*; Duggan, "Queering the State" and "Holy Matrimony!"; Card, "Against Marriage."

7. The exclusivity and value of the dissolution benefit were recently highlighted when the Rhode Island Supreme Court refused to allow a same-sex couple, married under Massachusetts law, to divorce in a Rhode Island court (Horton, "What's Tougher to Get Than a Same-sex Marriage?").

8. See, for example, Kennedy, "Ruling Clouds Inheritance of Rentals." For further elaboration, see Duggan, "Queering the State" and "Holy Matrimony!"; Fineman, *Neutered Mother*, chap. 6; Card, "Against Marriage"; Warner, *Trouble with Normal*, chap. 3; and Metz, "Liberal Case for Disestablishing Marriage."

9. In some states, able-bodied, two-parent families do not qualify for Temporary Assistance for Needy Families (TANF) benefits (Rowe et al., *Welfare Rules Datebook*, 18).

10. In *Marriage and Family*, see Amato, "Institutional, Companionate, and Individualistic Marriage," and Knox and Fein, "Supporting Healthy Marriage" for descriptions of these programs. See also *Healthy Marriage Initiative* of the Administration for Children and Families.

11. *Utah v. Green*. This contrasts with those who give no public title to their (multiple) sexual and childbearing unions and are left in most states, in practice and in technical legal terms, free to do as they choose. Though twenty-three states criminalize adultery, few actually enforce these laws, and legal scholars note a legal trend in the direction of decriminalizing adultery. See Falco, "The Road Not Taken," 743–46; Green, "Griswold's Legacy"; and Posner and Silbaugh, *A Guide to America's Sex Laws*, 98.

12. This has not always been the case, parents are not obligated to do much, and marriage is often treated as presumptive evidence of parenthood. Still, the state can and often does accomplish its role in enforcing some sort of parental obligation without the use of marriage. One obvious example is child support, which is required regardless of marital status (Smith, *Welfare Reform*, 2–4).

13. For example, *California Family Code* §297–299.6.

14. Coontz, *Marriage, a History*, 124; Stone, *Road to Divorce*, 133.
15. A. Ryan, "Liberalism."
16. Shklar, "Liberalism of Fear," 21.
17. For example, see Locke, *Second Treatise*; Mill, *Subjection of Women* and *On Liberty*; Shklar, "Liberalism of Fear"; Rawls, *Theory of Justice* and *Political Liberalism*; and Cornell, *At the Heart of Freedom*. With respect to family life, this approach recommends that the physical and material well-being of families, not marriage per se, be the measure of our family policy.
18. For example, Rawls, *Justice as Fairness*, 3.
19. Stone, *Road to Divorce*, 51–52, 133; Hartog, *Man and Wife in America*, 32; Cott, *Public Vows*, 9–11; Coontz, *Marriage, a History*, 2, 7.
20. For example, see Harriet Taylor, "Early Essay on Marriage"; Friedan, *Feminine Mystique*; Rich, "Compulsory Heterosexuality"; MacKinnon, *Feminism Unmodified*; Okin, *Justice, Gender, and the Family*; and Card, "Against Marriage."
21. This is a key difference between what Rawls calls political societies and communities. Rawls, *Justice as Fairness*, 21.
22. I engage liberalism in part because I am convinced that its values are worth promoting but also because we live in a liberal world. In the twenty-first century, democracy and, perhaps, theocracy stand as viable ways of organizing political life. Liberalism and democracy, it has been said, exist in something of a monogamous marriage. I, therefore, engage liberalism critically. This is not an attempt to bolster liberalism out of blind faith. Nor is it an attempt to make liberalism a perfectly coherent, comprehensive, and complete political theory. On this, I side with Isaiah Berlin: the demands of the individual and the community, of liberty and equality, unity and diversity, the right and the good cannot be flawlessly squared. At best, they can be balanced.
23. Fineman calls this "derivative dependency" (*Neutered Mother*, 8).
24. I am not the first contemporary scholar to recommend that we abolish marriage as a legal category. Feminist legal theorist Martha Fineman and queer theorists such as Claudia Card and Michael Warner are pioneers on this count. And our company grows.
25. Increasing numbers of scholars, policy makers, jurists, and the general public have weighed in on this issue. For example, see *In re Marriage Cases*; New Hampshire H.B. 0437; Caregiver Assistance and Relief Effort (CARE) Act; Fineman, *Neutered Mother* and *Autonomy Myth*; Peters and Kamp Dush, *Marriage and Family*; Shanley, *Just Marriage*; McClain, *Place of Families*; and Eichner, "Marriage and the Elephant."

26. Cott, *Public Vows*, 3–8; Coontz, *Marriage, a History*, 9.

27. Stone, *Road to Divorce*, 25.

28. I use "political theory" in its broadest sense, one that might include contemporary thinkers as diverse as Leo Strauss (see, for example, "Political Philosophy and History"), John Rawls (for example, *Justice as Fairness*, 1–5), Quentin Skinner (as, for example, in "The Idea of Negative Liberty"), Judith Shklar (in "What Is the Use of Utopia?"), and James Tully (in, for example, "Political Philosophy as a Critical Activity").

29. I am aware and wary of the distinct possibility that moving as quickly as I do from philosophy to policy, all in the language of philosophy, I run the risk of effacing the politics of my enterprise. I have tried to reduce this risk by flagging the politics.

30. Rawls, *Justice as Fairness*, 3; Shklar, "Utopia," 189; Tully, "Political Philosophy."

31. See Duggan, "Queering the State" and "Holy Matrimony!"; Shanley, *Just Marriage*; McClain, *Place of Families*; Fineman, *Neutered Mother*; and Shell, "Liberal Case against Gay Marriage." More broadly, the book contributes to the burgeoning conversation among contemporary political theorists about dependency, family, and intimate caregiving (McClain, *Place of Families*; Fineman, *Neutered Mother* and *Autonomy Myth*; Tronto, *Moral Boundaries*; Kittay, *Love's Labor*).

32. See Okin, Pateman, Fineman, and Elshtain.

33. See Rawls, Cornell, Allen, Minow, Shanley, and McClain.

34. See Okin, *Justice, Gender, and the Family*; Nussbaum, *Sex and Social Justice*; Deveaux, *Cultural Pluralism*; Spinner-Halev, *Surviving Diversity*; Shachar, *Multicultural Jurisdictions*; and Arneil et al., *Sexual Justice/Cultural Justice*.

CHAPTER TWO
CONFUSION IN THE COURTS

1. Rawls, *Theory of Justice*, §4, §9; *Justice as Fairness*, §9–10.

2. See, for example, Dworkin, *Law's Empire* and *Freedom's Law*; Scalia, *Matter of Interpretation*; and Rawls, *Justice as Fairness*, §9.3–9.4.

3. *Maynard v. Hill*, 213, citing *Noel v. Ewing*, 49–50.

4. This book is not intended to provide a comprehensive, up-to-the-minute analysis of American jurisprudence and debates concerning marriage. The goal here, in chapter 2, is simply to identify the tensions and confusions that need to be addressed if we wish to craft a coherent liberal theory and policy of marriage/state relations.

5. Many legal scholars see here a trend in American law toward a privileging of the individual over the familial unit, marital institution, and/

or society at large. See, for example, Brinig, "Supreme Court's Impact"; Schneider, "Moral Discourse"; Singer, "Privatization of Family Law"; and Regan, *Family Law and the Pursuit of Intimacy*. Citing *Maynard* and *Zablocki* as bookends, Singer writes that the Supreme Court shows the effect of a "doctrinal shift from family privacy to decisional autonomy" ("Privatization of Family Law," 1510). Yet in the most recent cases (e.g., *Zablocki* and *In re Marriage Cases*), the privacy claim is matched by a substantive due-process argument. Crucially, both tacks rely on a description of marriage not as a right but as an institution (see *Zablocki v. Redhail*, 384). More importantly, Singer's analysis cannot explain or make much sense of this back and forth. I want to argue that this back and forth reflects a tension that troubles all the cases and remains unresolved—and so provokes a schizophrenic treatment of marriage. The unresolved question is why the state should control and use *marriage as such*.

6. *Maynard v. Hill*, 210–13, citing *Wade v. Kalbfleisch*, 282, 284.

7. Note that this is not an anachronistic question: ten years earlier, the Supreme Court handed down the seminal *Reynolds* case outlawing one—the polygamist—version of the institution. As we shall see shortly, the Court's tack in this case illustrates how far it was from finding a way to reconcile its views of marriage and its liberal commitments to the limited state.

8. *Reynolds v. United States*, 7.

9. And yet, perhaps because of deep and widespread consensus condemning polygamy and supporting state control of marriage, *Reynolds* continues to be cited as precedent. See, for example, *Utah v. Green* and *Utah v. Holm*.

10. *Reynolds v. United States*, 41.

11. In fact, Waite felt little need to prove that polygamous marriage is an act. He wrote that a subsidiary question the Court would address was whether religious belief could excuse an individual from culpability for "an overt act made criminal by the law of the land" (ibid., 162). In other words, he saw plural marriage as an act, pure and simple.

12. Polygamy, Waite wrote, was widely considered "odious among the northern and western nations of Europe, and, until the establishment of the Mormon Church, was almost exclusively a feature of the life of Asiatic and of African people. . . . From the earliest history of England polygamy has been treated as an offence [*sic*] against society" (ibid., 164). In light of this history, the justice explained, it is clear that the founders did not intend to protect polygamy.

13. Ibid., 35–38.

14. Ibid., 165–66.

15. Ibid., 40.

16. Ibid.

17. Lieber was a well-known and influential legal theorist in nineteenth-century America (Cott, *Public Vows*, 114). On this particular question, Lieber was influenced by Hegel's *Philosophy of Right*; see Strassberg, "Distinctions of Form or Substance."

18. *Reynolds v. United States*, 166.

19. *Meyer v. Nebraska*, 399.

20. *Skinner v. Oklahoma*, 541.

21. *Loving v. Virginia*, 10.

22. *Zablocki v. Redhail*, 383; see, for example, *Utah v. Green*; *In re Marriage Cases*, 49; and the line of cases that culminates in *Zablocki*: *Loving v. Virginia*, *Skinner v. Oklahoma*, and *Meyer v. Nebraska*.

23. Locke, *Second Treatise*, §123 (350).

24. Lévi-Strauss, "The Family," 270.

25. To be sure, those rights too must be defined; and, in fact, legal battles are fought over those definitions: what is pornography, speech, conscience, religion, and so forth. The relevant difference is that being married involves assuming a status defined by forces outside those who assume it.

26. *Griswold v. Connecticut*, 486.

27. *Eisenstadt v. Baird*, 454.

28. *Wade v. Kalbfleisch*, 285.

29. *Maynard v. Hill*, 212–13.

30. In theory, the cases of the 1940s, 1950s, and 1960s that challenged antimiscegenation laws raised similar questions. Whether because of the evolution of legal discourse concerning marriage or differences between the ways race and sexual orientation were seen with respect to marriage, the courts of that period focused more on rights and privacy than on the institution.

31. *Opinions of the Justices*, 1211.

32. *Goodridge v. Dept. of Public Health*, 27.

33. *In re Marriage Cases*, 801–9. See the California Domestic Partner Rights and Responsibilities Act of 2003.

34. *In re Marriage Cases*, 780.

35. Ibid., 811.

36. Ibid., 818–19.

37. Ibid., 819.

38. Ibid., 812–13.

39. For example, ibid., 815–16, 830, etc.

40. Ibid., 814–15.

41. Ibid., 819–20, emphasis mine.

42. Ibid., 815–18.

43. Ibid., n11.

44. Ibid., 813–14, emphasis original.

45. Ibid., 818–19, emphasis original.

46. One way to read the court's position is that the right to marry functions as a trump card that nothing—for example, concerns about diversity—could override. So hints the "fundamental" designation. But, as the court's own caution in emphasizing the civil goods of marriage suggests, all rights, fundamental or otherwise, must conform to the basic liberal democratic principles girding the Constitution. (With time, the right to private property could not protect slavery. The right to contract could not protect business owners' unequal power over their employees.) It would, of course, be misleading to suggest that there is an uncomplicated test by which to check whether practices meet these standards. Nor is it accurate to suggest that "liberal democratic" principles are perfectly definable and never in tension with each other. But still, as the court's caution suggests, even fundamental rights must conform in some plausible way to some plausible interpretation of these principles filtered through the relevant constitutions.

47. *In re Marriage Cases*, 779.

48. Ibid., 781.

49. Ibid., 781–82.

50. Ibid., 830, emphasis original.

Chapter Three
Marriage and the State in Liberal Political Thought

1. This is not to say that most liberal political philosophers ignore marriage altogether, but rather that they tend to consider the institution only in passing. Immanuel Kant, Alexis de Toqueville, and Rawls are examples of such thinkers. John Milton, Mary Wollstonecraft, and Wilhelm von Humboldt are more like Locke, Mill, and Okin in their sustained critical analysis of marriage.

2. Important differences notwithstanding, Locke, Mill, and Okin are undisputed representatives of the liberal political tradition; Locke and Mill have been called "patron saints of liberalism" for their defenses of individual freedom and limited government (Shklar, "Liberalism of Fear," 9). Unlike most of their philosophical compatriots, they focus express critical attention on marriage, and especially on gender relations within it. Their treatments of marriage are the liberal canon's most sophisticated and, thus, the ones most deserving of attention.

3. Shanley, "Marriage Contract," 90, 93–94; Butler, "Early Liberal Roots," 81–90; Locke, *Second Treatise*, n. to §78 (319).

4. See Pateman, *Sexual Contract*, 21, 54; Shanley, "Marriage Contract," 93; Butler, "Early Liberal Roots," 81–82 and 88–90; and Okin, *Women in Western Political Thought*, 199–201.

5. Unless otherwise noted, I draw the present description of the political context and discourse within which Locke wrote from Shanley, "Marriage Contract"; Butler, "Early Liberal Roots"; and Stone, *Road to Divorce*.

6. Shanley, "Marriage Contract," 85.

7. Ibid., 81, 84; Stone, *Road to Divorce*, 1–2.

8. Shanley, "Marriage Contract," 80–81.

9. Ibid., 80–82.

10. Before Locke presented his argument in *Two Treatises of Government*, antiroyalist attempts to secure the marital metaphor to their advantage foundered on both points. They were victims of their unwillingness to draw out the radical implications that their views of human freedom and equality would have for marriage. James Tyrrell, Locke's liberal-in-arms, for example, denied the permissibility of divorce, despite his vigorous defense of the revolutionary implications of his contractarian logic in the realm of politics—that the relationship between king and subjects had to be based on voluntary consent and was, therefore, determinable and dissoluble. See Shanley, "Marriage Contract," 89–90.

11. Locke, *Second Treatise*, §78 (319).

12. Ibid., §81 (321).

13. Ibid., §83 (322).

14. Shanley contends that it was not logic alone that drove Locke to make this argument. Rather, it was primarily his concern with overturning the patriarchalists' use of the marriage contract in their political rhetoric that led Locke to articulate a defense of divorce ("Marriage Contract," 81). Laslett, however, in his editorial notes to *Second Treatise*, suggests that Locke was convinced by the logic of his position and, in fact, was willing, at least in private, to extend it even further (Locke, *Second Treatise*, n. to §81.5–7 [321]). According to Okin, Mill often "played down or omitted his radical ideas about divorce" for prudential reasons (*Women in Western Political Thought*, 203).

15. Locke, *Second Treatise*, §81 (321).

16. Laslett in Locke, *Second Treatise*, n. to §81.5–7 (321).

17. Stone, *Road to Divorce*, 1–2.

18. Laslett, "Introduction," 44.

19. Shanley, "Marriage Contract," 95.

20. Locke, *Second Treatise*, §123 (350).

21. Locke, *Letter*, 26. Civil jurisdiction "reaches only to these Civil Concernments; and that all Civil Power, Right and Dominion, is bounded

and confined to the only care of promoting these things; and that it neither can nor ought in any manner to be extended to the Salvation of Souls" (Locke, *Letter*, 26).

22. Creppell, "Locke on Toleration," 225. See also Shanley, "Marriage Contract," 94–95; Elshtain, *Public Man, Private Woman*, 116–27.

23. Locke, *Letter*, 34.

24. Locke, *Second Treatise*, §80 (320).

25. Ibid., §79 (319).

26. Ibid., §83 (321–22).

27. Ibid., §123–24 (350).

28. Ibid., §89 (325).

29. Regan defines "status" as "the notion that family members [have] specific legal identities that [are] the source of relatively fixed rights and obligations" and as "a legal identity that is subject to a set of publicly imposed expectations largely independent of the preferences of the person who holds that status" (*Family Law*, 6, 9).

30. Locke, *Second Treatise*, §83 (322).

31. Locke, *Letter*, 33.

32. Locke, *Second Treatise*, §81–82 (321).

33. See, for example, Strauss, *Natural Right*, 202–51.

34. Fineman, *Autonomy Myth*, 33–37, and *Neutered Mother*, 161–63; Kittay, *Love's Labor*, 29–48.

35. Locke, *Second Treatise*, §78 (319).

36. These omissions would have been noticeable to his contemporaries—as they later were to Elrington—because marriage was so widely understood as a fundamentally religious institution (Stone, *Road to Divorce*, 1–2). Even though the Anglican Church rejected the Catholic tenet that marriage was a sacrament, most English people considered marriage to be a sacred union with wider social, religious, and psychological significance than, say, a business partnership (Stone, *Road to Divorce*, 16), though most also considered it to be something of an economic partnership (Stone, *Road to Divorce*, 6).

37. Locke, *Second Treatise*, §58 (306–7), §78 (319), §80 (320), §83 (321–22).

38. It is worth noting the problem with Locke's argument here. An obligation of care cannot justify the state's enforcing a prepolitically defined marital status. Why? First, care of children can be achieved outside marriage. There is no intrinsic connection between marriage and the reproduction or care of children. It is not, of course, surprising that Locke would not endorse such a practice. Nonetheless, experience shows that it can be done. To say that the state must ensure that the natural duty of care

of one's offspring is met is, therefore, to say nothing of its right or duty to enforce a particular marital status. Second, the obligation to care for one's offspring does not, even according to Locke, hinge on marital status. According to Locke, parental obligation is natural and common to all species (*Second Treatise*, §79–80 [319–20]). Similarly, the state's role in securing property arrangements stands, regardless of the marital status of an individual—at least according to the logic of his argument. Even if Locke's liberal state must be concerned with protecting children and securing property, this does not justify state enforcement of a divinely defined marital status.

39. Fineman, *Neutered Mother*; Folbre, *Invisible Heart* and *Valuing Children*; Kittay, *Love's Labor*; Metz, "Liberal Case for Disestablishing Marriage," 209–10; Tronto, *Moral Boundaries*.

40. Fineman, *Neutered Mother*, 8, 161–64.

41. Of course, caregiving also produces unique, priceless rewards that most caregivers would not quickly give up. Unfortunately—to paraphrase the Harvard janitorial union—one cannot eat these kinds of rewards (Gould-Wartofsky, "Too Cruel").

42. For a thoughtful discussion on this matter, see Regan, *Family Law*; see also Metz, "Liberal Case for Disestablishing Marriage"; Shanley, *Just Marriage*; McClain, *Place of Families*; Fineman, *Autonomy Myth* and *Neutered Mother*.

43. Shanley, *Just Marriage*, 26–28.

44. Mill, *On Liberty*, 49.

45. Okin, *Women in Western Political Thought*, 195–230; Shanley, "Marital Slavery."

46. For example, see Mill, *On Liberty*, 48.

47. Ibid., 122.

48. Mill, *Subjection of Women*, 233–35.

49. Mill, *Early Essays*, 72.

50. Mill, *Subjection of Women*, 169.

51. Mill, *On Liberty*, 121–22.

52. Mill, "Early Essay," 80–84; *On Liberty*, 121–22; and *Subjection of Women*, 161.

53. Mill, *On Liberty*, 122.

54. Taylor, "Early Essay," 86–87.

55. Ibid., 85.

56. Humboldt, *Limits of State Action*, 31.

57. Humboldt is not unconcerned with the social functions associated with marriage. Rather, he believes that individual and societal interests around children and intimate care are more likely to coincide when

individuals are left unfettered by state action (see Humboldt, *Limits of State Action*, 31). Humboldt's naïve optimism on this count highlights the problems with the libertarian case for disestablishing marriage: as Mill's response suggests, it completely ignores how the combination of value and risks inherent in intimate caregiving gives the state good reason to provide some sort of insurance, in the form of a status, for those who opt to engage in relatively stable, relatively long-term intimate caregiving unions, marital or otherwise.

58. Humboldt, *Limits of State Action*, 95.

59. Mill does consider meaning and the constitutive effect of laws when discussing what the content of marriage law ought to be. These issues do not, however, factor into or contribute to reasons he presents that might justify state control and use of marital status in the first place. Mill notes that his discussion in *On Liberty* is inadequate to the subject. My point is that even his considerations in *The Subjection of Women* do not provide adequate backing for his position that the state should recognize and regulate marriage as such.

60. Mill, *On Liberty*, 48–49.

61. Note that this seems more extreme than Locke, who includes life, liberty, and property, even the common good, in the purview of the state. In fact, however, Mill extends harm quite far—to a point that leads many to doubt the use of the measure. For all of its problems, the harm principle has been given long life, at least in American jurisprudence. See, for example, *Schenck v. United States*; *Dennis v. United States*.

62. Mill, *On Liberty*, 122.

63. Ibid.

64. Ibid., 123.

65. Ibid.

66. Ibid., 126.

67. Mill, *Subjection of Women*, 163.

68. Mill, *On Liberty*, chap. 2.

69. Ibid., 121.

70. Ibid., 126.

71. Ibid., 122–24, 126.

72. Okin, *Justice, Gender, and the Family*, 135–36.

73. Ibid., 138 (emphasis original).

74. Mill, *Subjection of Women*, chap. 4.

75. Okin, *Justice, Gender, and the Family*, 147 (emphasis original).

76. Ibid., 180.

77. Ibid., 180–81 (emphasis original).

78. Ibid., 170.

79. Ibid., 180.

80. Ibid., 169.

81. See Rawls, *Political Liberalism* and *Theory of Justice*; Kittay, *Love's Labor*; and Okin, *Justice, Gender, and the Family.*

CHAPTER FOUR

MARRIAGE: A FORMAL, COMPREHENSIVE SOCIAL INSTITUTION

1. Scholars have long abandoned efforts to craft a universal definition of marriage. See, for example, Coontz, *Marriage, a History*, 24–33; Leach, "Polyandry," 183; and Thornton, "Comparative and Historical Perspectives," 588, 600–1.

2. Here, I draw on the concept/conception distinction that John Rawls uses in *A Theory of Justice* to distinguish between the general idea of justice and particular, substantive views of it (*Theory of Justice*, 4–6, following Hart, *Concept of Law*). Also see Gallie, "Essentially Contested Concepts."

3. Schneider, "Channeling Function," 529–32.

4. See Cruz, " 'Just Don't Call It Marriage' " and "Disestablishing Sex and Gender"; Glendon, *Abortion and Divorce*; Schneider, "Channeling Function"; and Card, "Against Marriage" and "Gay Divorce."

5. Cruz, " 'Just Don't Call It Marriage,' " 933.

6. Ibid., 928.

7. *Goodridge v. Dept. of Public Health*, 322.

8. Shanley, *Just Marriage*, 6.

9. Cruz, " 'Just Don't Call It Marriage,' " 934–35.

10. Cruz acknowledges this difficulty but argues, first, that "social and civil marriage are intertwined and cannot be so easily divorced (no pun intended)," and second, that "social marriage . . . powerfully relies on civil marriage: most people who marry civilly without any church ceremony and then hold themselves out as married are, I wager, treated socially as married largely on account of their civil marriage" (ibid., n40). As I argue above, this wager about the way things are explains neither why they are so nor whether they must be.

11. *Opinions of the Justices*, 1211.

12. Glendon, *Abortion and Divorce*, 7–9.

13. Ibid., 9.

14. *Reynolds v. United States*, 165–66.

15. Rauch, "Family Reunion" (available only online).

16. *Utah v. Holm*, 56; crucially, this assertion allows the court, unsuccessfully I believe, to skirt the defendant's position that his behavior—

the actual actions—is protected because it is private in precisely the same sense as were Lawrence's actions in the landmark *Lawrence v. Texas.*

17. Schneider, "Channeling Function," 498, citing Bellah et al., *Good Society,* 10. Schneider argues that, although it may be best to speak of them "merely [as] analytic constructs," it is still not "pointless" to speak of social institutions (499–500).

18. Ibid., 498.

19. Ibid., 504, citing Berger and Luckmann, *Social Construction,* 52.

20. See, for instance, Card, "Against Marriage," 6–7.

21. Cornell, *At the Heart of Freedom,* 7.

22. Okin, *Justice, Gender, and the Family,* 135–36. Cornell argues that "the promotion of the integrity of heterosexual monogamous marriage in a politically liberal society is illegitimate because it violates the sanctuary of personality, the imaginary domain" (*At the Heart of Freedom,* 39). See Warner, *Trouble with Normal,* 81–147; marriage, he argues, is a fiercely normalizing institution, and not only for those in it. He thus bemoans the fact that with the gay, same-sex-marriage campaign, "the queer critique of sexual normalization and state regulation simply disappear" (95). Card warns that legal marriage simply provides the state with a powerful mechanism for regulating intimate life ("Against Marriage," 6–7).

23. Schneider, "Channeling Function," 504.

24. Card, "Against Marriage," 1–2; Schneider, "Channeling Function," 500.

25. Hegel may seem an odd choice to turn to for insight concerning marriage and the state in liberal theory and practice. He is, after all, one of liberalism's most forceful critics. Still, he is an appropriate source for our inquiry. First, like any critic, he shares assumptions and commitments with those he interrogates. Like the liberals he takes to task, Hegel is committed to securing individual autonomy in the context of a complex, modern polity. Thus, his thoughts on marriage and the state share something of a common foundation with those of the liberal theorists and legal systems we investigate. Second, public recognition and its role in reproducing public meaning, affecting individual self-understanding and developing ties between individuals and their community, are central to his analysis of how marriage helps overcome what he sees as modernity's independence-interdependence paradox. See Strassberg, "Distinctions of Form."

26. To anticipate concerns, let me state from the outset that I shall argue that we may be convinced by Hegel's explanation of the transformative potential of marriage and the role of public control of the institution in the production of this potential, yet not be bound to accept his views

about women or, crucially for our purposes, his idea that the *state* must control marital status in order for its extra value to be realized (Pateman, *Sexual Contract*, 173–81). We can and should reject both these elements of Hegel's account and still gain useful lessons from his description of the functions of public definition and conferral of marital status.

27. This marriage must be monogamous because the goods of marriage require total, mutual "surrender." It must be heterosexual because one of the differences it overcomes is sexual. It must be consented to by both parties, and it must be publicly recognized.

Hegel argues that marriage integrates individuals with each other and with their community on three levels. First, the institution helps generate trust and deep identification from the "inside out"—from the depths of self-consciousness to public personae—between two individuals. It does so by offering a handicap against the risk inherent in love, in a setting that celebrates subjective emotional and sexual desire. (See *Philosophy of Right*, A to §158 [261–62], §162 [111], §167 [115].) Second, marriage facilitates integration by providing a powerful emotional experience of "rational" trust between individuals. This, Hegel argues, can serve as a model for more generalized trust that transfers to relationships with other citizens and to the institutions of social and political life. (See ibid., 422.) Third, because marriage (and the community that recognizes and regulates it) provides the material and meaning context within which the individual experiences a sort of safe integration with another human being, Hegel argues, those individuals come to appreciate that their freedom and happiness are integrally tied to these institutions and the recognizing community; and, therefore, they develop deep affection and trust for them. (See ibid., A to §265 [281]). For a more detailed discussion of Hegel on marriage, see Metz, "Liberal Case for Disestablishing Marriage."

28. Carole Pateman argues that, for Hegel, the gap between individual wills is overcome at the cost of nullifying female will. The original standpoint of contract is overcome because the female will essentially becomes a nonentity after the initial consent. How, Pateman rightly asks, could this arrangement respect the principle of subjectivity? Hegel's claim that it does stems, she argues, from his desire to obscure the "sexual contract" upon which his and most other Western political theories are based (*Sexual Contract*, 176–81). While she is right to identify Hegel's contradictory and problematic views on women, Pateman's exclusive focus on these features of his argument causes her to miss Hegel's story of psychological integration and, especially illuminating for our purposes, his compelling explanation of how the political community's involvement as a third party to the conjugal contract produces a socializing experience that makes the contract obsolete.

29. Hegel, *Philosophy of Right*, §163 (112). Marriage begins in contract to honor subjectivity and individual choice, but contract is not enough. Marriage that stayed at the level of contract would amount to little more than an economic partnership and thus generate a desiccated sense of commitment. Marital relations are about something above the alienation and arbitrariness of econo-contract relations. To overcome the dilemma at the heart of modern freedom, between individuality and the necessity of interdependence, marriage must produce a sense of obligation that is not experienced as such—it must seem like the natural thing to do. Hence, subsuming marriage under the concept of contract, Hegel explains, threatens to leave its adherents with a superficial sense of obligation to one another. (See *Philosophy of Right*, §75 [58–59], A to §161 [262], §162 [111], and §163 [112–13].)

30. Ibid., §77 (59–60), A to §71 (242), and §211–18 (134–40).

31. For example, see ibid., §71 (57) and §217–18 (139–40).

32. Ibid., §78 (60).

33. Hegel's note: "The fact that the church comes in in this connexion is a further point, but not one for discussion here" (Ibid., §164 [113]). Here, the translator directs readers to §270 (164–74), a treatise on the relation between church and state, the major gist of which is thus: if religion is genuine—really connected to or reflecting absolute truth—then it does not run counter to the ethical state. Rather, it supports the state. This reading is confirmed by the translator's notes 10–12 (365).

34. Ibid., §164 (113).

35. Ibid., §176 (118); n30 (352).

36. Ibid., §164 (113–14).

37. Ibid., A to §176 (265).

38. Anthropologist Claude Lévi-Strauss notes that, in every society, marriage is, and in fact must be, a public matter: "whatever the way in which the collectivity expresses its interest in the marriage of its members . . . it remains true that marriage is not, is never, and cannot be a private business" ("The Family," 270).

39. Geertz, "Religion as a Cultural System," 94–98.

40. Lehmann-Haupt, "Need a Minister?"

41. Universal Life Church Monastery, http://www.ulcordination .org/.

42. Lehmann-Haupt notes the reasons that people gave her for choosing this option: "The large number of interfaith couples; the desire to be married by someone loving and close rather than by an impersonal official; and some couples' conviction that they have less need of the imprimatur of a religious authority and instead draw their sense of community from their own circle" ("Need a Minister?," 1).

43. Ibid.

44. Ibid., 8.

45. *Reynolds v. United States*, 165–66.

46. Hegel influenced Lieber on the subject of the connection between marriage and political life, hence the similarities between Lieber and Hegel are not surprising (see Strassberg, "Distinctions of Form," 1523). See also Cook and Leavelle, "German Idealism," 221; and Robson, "Francis Lieber's Theories," 231.

CHAPTER FIVE

THE LIBERAL CASE FOR DISESTABLISHING MARRIAGE
AND CREATING AN INTIMATE CAREGIVING UNION STATUS

1. Rauch, "Family Reunion."

2. For example, see Locke, *Second Treatise*; Mill, *On Liberty*; Berlin, *Four Essays*; Shklar, "Liberalism of Fear"; Rawls, *Theory of Justice, Political Liberalism*, and *Justice as Fairness*; Dworkin, *Taking Rights Seriously*; Van Parijs, *Real Freedom*; Cornell, *At the Heart of Freedom*; and Pettit, *Republicanism*.

3. It is important to note that a constitutive status differs from what we might call an instrumental-plus status, such as citizenship. It seems accurate to say the state intends to alter self-understanding when it confers citizenship status. And yet citizenship differs from Hegel's constitutive status on three important counts. First, its aim is narrowly limited to publicly known and, at least ostensibly, supported political purposes. Second, its object is limited to political self-understanding, as opposed to that of a constitutive status, which extends even to the "sexuate" self (Cornell, *At the Heart of Freedom*). Third, while affecting belief is clearly a purpose of citizenship status, it is not the primary purpose. Instrumental concerns provide the initial justification for the state's creation and use of the status. Thus, even an instrumental-plus status does not rely on the sort of ethical community assumed by a constitutive status.

4. Locke, *Letter*, 33.

5. Ibid., 26.

6. Ibid., 40.

7. Ibid., 27.

8. Jefferson, "Query XVII"; Madison, "Memorial and Remonstrance."

9. In his important book *Heart of Justice: A Political Theory of Caring*, Daniel Engster develops a similar justification for state support of care (including nonintimate). See, especially, 39–46.

10. Levy, "At the Intersection of Intimacy and Care," 72–73; Kittay, *Love's Labor*, 140–46; Tronto, *Moral Boundaries*, 161–70.

11. Stacey, "Toward Equal Regard for Marriages"; McClain, *Place of Families*; Peters and Kamp Dush, *Marriage and Family*.

12. See Gross, "Older Women Team Up." The question of whether groups of sexually intimate adults and their children should be considered intimate caregiving units is, in my view, quite simple. If they provide intimate care as described, then the answer is yes. Polygamous units may also be intimate caregiving units. I shall defend the possibility that these units receive support from the state. They are not, however, common enough to be included in this list. In any case, polygamous units are too provocative to include without explanation.

13. Simmons and O'Neill, *Households and Families: 2000*, 1, 3, 7. Although 68 percent of children live in married-parent households, this is 4 percent less than in 1990, signaling an increase in the percentage of children living in nonmarital households—whether single-parent, multigenerational, or with nonparent relatives or nonrelatives (Johnson et al., "Changes in the Lives of U.S. Children," 27).

14. Smith, *Welfare Reform*, 147–88.

15. Other scholars have written thoughtfully and more extensively on these matters. See, for example, Tronto, *Moral Boundaries*; Kittay, *Love's Labor*; Hirschmann, *Rethinking Obligation*; Levy, "At the Intersection of Intimacy and Care"; Fineman, *Neutered Mother* and *Autonomy Myth*; Smith, *Welfare Reform*; and McClain, *Place of Families*.

16. *Bowers v. Hardwick*, 1986; *Lawrence v. Texas*, 2003; Fineman, *Neutered Mother* and *Autonomy Myth*; Smith, *Welfare Reform*; Allen, *Uneasy Access*.

17. Elshtain, *Public Man, Private Woman*; Allen, *Uneasy Access*; MacKinnon, *Feminism Unmodified*; Eskow, "The Ultimate Weapon?"; Ryan, "Sex Right."

18. See Okin, *Justice, Gender, and the Family*; and Folbre, *Invisible Heart*.

19. Well aware of the dangers of this ideal, I rely on it still, for without an ideal, we have neither measure nor goal (see Shklar, "Utopia").

20. Bloom, *Republic of Plato*. To call the communist experiment of book 5 of the *Republic* a dystopia is not to say that it does not illustrate important "feminist" points about the connection between gender inequality and the social conventions of female primary caregiving, the segregation of public and private, and so on. It is merely to concur with Aristotle's assessment that one of the lessons to be gleaned from the experiment is that human beings take better care of what they perceive as "their own."

See Okin, *Women in Western Political Thought*, pts. 1–2; and Aristotle, *Politics*, bk. 2.3.

21. Okin, *Justice, Gender, and the Family*; Noddings, *Caring*; McClain, *Place of Families*.

22. Given the vast diversity of caregiving arrangements across history and geography, it seems hubristic to assume that 1950s America discovered the eternally and universally best arrangement. See Leach, "Polyandry" and *Rethinking Anthropology*; Bell, "Defining Marriage and Legitimacy"; and Borneman, "Until Death Do Us Part."

23. Cornell, *At the Heart of Freedom*.

24. Miller, *Toward a New Psychology*, 83–114; Noddings, *Caring*, 6, 51; Elshtain, *Public Man, Private Woman*, 326–30; McClain, *Place of Families*, 68–71.

25. Arendt, "Reflections on Little Rock," 55–56; Elshtain, *Public Man, Private Woman*, 330–31; McClain, *Place of Families*, 29–49; Smith, *Welfare Reform*, 56–58.

26. Elshtain, *Public Man, Private Woman*, 335; Arendt, "Reflections on Little Rock," 55–56.

27. In addition, to say that intimate care is especially valuable is not to deny the virtues of public care. There are many, and the state should support such care and ensure against its dangers. (It would, of course, be possible that most of the care I am describing could be provided publicly. And in fact, one might argue that care could and should be provided directly by the state, precisely to avoid the vulnerability and inequality caused by "private" caregiving. While this objection has some merit, it ignores the value of privacy, intimacy, and diversity in caregiving.)

28. My guess is that this is increasingly not true. In other words, there are plenty of signs, such as the rise of paid care for children, the infirm, and the elderly, that more and more of both survival and nurturance care takes place outside what I am describing as intimate caregiving relationships.

29. Fineman, *Neutered Mother*, 161–64; Folbre, *Invisible Heart*, 22–52; Tronto, *Moral Boundaries*, 109–20; Kittay, *Love's Labor*, 33–37, 46–48; Okin, *Justice, Gender, and the Family*, 134–41.

30. See Folbre, *Invisible Heart*. For our purposes, the difference between paid and unpaid caregiving is important. Without denying that paid caregivers are typically underpaid and underprotected by the law, the employment contract and delineated terms of remuneration guard the paid caregiver from the risks of her labor in ways that do not exist for the unpaid caregiver.

31. Martha Fineman persuasively shows that when the state uses marital status as the primary avenue through which to support caregiving,

it significantly disadvantages many actual caregivers. Social-welfare policies aimed at discouraging unwed, single motherhood are powerful examples of this dynamic. Not only do such policies perpetuate the view that single motherhood is bad in itself, but they actually make it more difficult to be a successful single mother (*Neutered Mother*, 100–42).

32. In his chapter in *Marriage and Family*, Steven Nock sketches one way in which the social significance of marriage is changing. However, he does not address alternative ways that people might express elements of the message he attributes to marriage. For instance, I suspect that, with time, civil union will carry many similar connotations of responsibility and commitment.

33. Blankenhorn, *Future of Marriage*; Waite and Gallagher, *Case for Marriage*; Shell, "Liberal Case against Gay Marriage"; Elshtain, "Feminism, Family, and Community"; Galston, "Divorce American Style" and "Reinstitutionalization of Marriage."

34. Here, it is appropriate to address claims based in social science that marriage makes adults and children healthier, wealthier, and happier. Such arguments—most forcefully and comprehensively expressed in Waite and Gallagher's *The Case for Marriage*—are flawed for a number of reasons. The most significant problem with this research is that when social scientists measure the effects of *marriage*, they are in fact measuring the effects of a wide and not entirely identifiable collection of influencing factors. Thus, they cannot say whether the apparent benefits of being married come from the legal benefits, the social approbation attached to the title, or an effect of self-selection. Identifying the specific causal factors matters because, for instance, if a key reason that married people do better is the concrete civil benefits they receive, such benefits could be spread easily to others without going through marriage. If their success has to do with the social approbation their status brings, again, we ought to think of ways of spreading the title around and have it come from effective ethical authorities. As it is, social science has not answered these questions (they may be impossible to answer with the kind of specificity required by social science) and thus ought not to be pulled out as the trump card as it is in many contemporary debates.

35. *Defense of Marriage Act*; Blankenhorn, *Future of Marriage*; Shell, "Liberal Case against Gay Marriage."

36. See Shanley, *Just Marriage*, and McClain, *Place of Families*.

37. Stacey, "Toward Equal Regard for Marriages"; Shanley, *Just Marriage*; McClain, *Place of Families*.

38. For scholars who call for the abolition of marriage as a legal category, see Fineman, *Neutered Mother*; Duggan, "Queering the State"

and "Holy Matrimony!"; Card, "Against Marriage"; Warner, *Trouble with Normal*; and Metz, "Liberal Case for Disestablishing Marriage."

39. See McClain, *Place of Families*; Shanley, *Just Marriage*; and Minow and Shanley, "Relational Rights and Responsibilities."

40. Pateman, *Sexual Contract*.

41. Lehman and Phelps, *West's Encyclopedia of American Law*, 479.

42. See Smith, *Welfare Reform*, for an account of the ills of the unprotected privacy of poor families.

43. *Goodridge v. Dept. of Public Health*, 1.

44. Rauch, "Family Reunion."

45. Shanley, *Just Marriage*, 6, 16.

46. Metz, "Liberal Case for Disestablishing Marriage."

47. To the extent that the proposed regime spreads support to intimate caregiving in its various forms, this approach is flexible enough to catch the positive potential in the current experimentation. Therefore, it would do better than "marriage" does in realizing the legitimate public-welfare goals of supporting intimate caregiving.

48. See, for example, Weitzman, *The Divorce Revolution*, and Sugarman and Hill Kay, *Divorce Reform*, on the importance of such provisions in no-fault divorce legislation.

49. See Farson, *Birthrights*; Minow, "Rights and Relations" and "Rights for the Next Generation"; Freeman, *Children's Rights*; and Purdy, *In Their Best Interest?*

50. Fineman, "Why Marriage?," 48. Also see Morriss, "How to Think about Marriage."

51. Fineman, *Neutered Mother*, 229.

52. See *Griswold v. Connecticut*, 1965; *Loving v. Virginia*, 1967; *Zablocki v. Redhail*, 1978; *Bowers v. Hardwick*, 1986; and Cornell, *At the Heart of Freedom*.

53. *Utah v. Green*, 2001.

54. Derbyshire, "Britney's Wedding."

55. Goodstein, "Gay Couples Seek Union"; Crampton, "Rabbi Isn't Fazed by Legalities."

56. Mankiw, *Principles of Macroeconomics*, 486.

57. I do not assume that these other sources of ethical authority are wholly positive. Many communal authorities will, no doubt, as they do now, promote unjust marital arrangements. However, just as we do not outlaw traditional marriage because it is unjust, I aim to show that the benefits of releasing "marriage" to communal authorities outweigh the costs of not doing so. The regime I propose actually makes it easier for

the state to protect individuals against unjust arrangements than is currently the case.

58. *Defense of Marriage Act*, sec. 7.

59. A classic account of the dangers of traditional, gendered marriage is in Okin, *Justice, Gender, and the Family*. See also England, "Gender Perspective on Marriage."

60. I am tempted to resist the label "single" for the following reason: single implies alone or isolated. But single people too need—and typically do procure—intimate care. What makes us "single" is that we gain and give this care in informal and irregular relationships. Forced to be creative and continually aware of their potential vulnerability, so-called single people probably find and cultivate a much wider array of intimate caregiving sources than nonsingle people. In a society dominated by the ideal of the sexually exclusive, long-term intimate relationship, these facts are easy to miss. This said, I recognize that intimate care gained in this multipronged, less regularized, and wholly unregulated fashion may be less secure and certainly requires more energy than most other approaches.

61. Locke, *Second Treatise*, §3 (268).

CHAPTER SIX
RECONSIDERING THE PUBLIC/PRIVATE DIVIDE

1. See Okin, *Is Multiculturalism Bad for Women?*; Nussbaum, *Sex and Social Justice*; Deveaux, *Cultural Pluralism*; Spinner-Halev, *Surviving Diversity*; Shachar, *Multicultural Jurisdictions*; and Arneil et al., *Sexual Justice/Cultural Justice*.

2. For a discussion of these issues, see Deveaux, *Cultural Pluralism*.

3. Locke, *Second Treatise*; Mill, *Subjection of Women* and *On Liberty*; Shklar, "Liberalism of Fear"; Rawls, *Theory of Justice*, *Political Liberalism*, and *Justice as Fairness*.

4. Shklar, "Liberalism of Fear," 6–7.

5. See, for example, Mill, Elshtain, Okin, Pateman, Sandel, and Brown.

6. Mill, *Subjection of Women* and *On Liberty*; Elshtain, *Public Man, Private Woman*; Okin, *Women in Western Political Thought* and *Justice, Gender, and the Family*; Pateman, *Disorder of Women* and *Sexual Contract*; MacKinnon, *Feminism Unmodified*; Olsen, "Myth of State Intervention."

7. Deep differences notwithstanding, all feminists took or take the public/private divide—its reality and its illusion—to be central to under-

standing power in liberal polities and theory—and, of course, marriage. Indeed, Carole Pateman identifies this focus as defining of feminism itself: "The dichotomy between the private and the public is central to almost two centuries of feminist writing and political struggle; it is, ultimately, what the feminist movement is about" (*Disorder of Women*, 18).

8. Olsen, "Myth of State Intervention."

9. My claim is not that thinkers such as Okin wish to do away with the public/private distinction altogether. Rather, it is that this conclusion might seem to follow from her criticism. If the divide is to be saved, the implicit challenge must be addressed more fully than it is by Okin and other liberal feminists.

10. Shklar, "Liberalism of Fear," 6.

11. Administration for Children and Families, *Healthy Marriage Initiative*.

12. Bennhold, "A Veil Closes France's Door to Citizenship."

13. For example, see *Nicomachean Ethics*, 1.3.

14. For some of the best recent literature on the importance of judgment in politics and political theory, see Frank, *Democracy of Distinction*; Garsten, *Saving Persuasion*; and Steinberger, *Concept of Political Judgment*.

15. As Geuss puts it, "There is no such thing as *the* public/private distinction, or, at any rate, it is a deep mistake to think that there is a single substantive distinction here that can be made to do any real philosophical or political work. . . . This does not *in itself* mean that any particular thing—object, institution, feature of human life, and so on—that is now valued as a special public or private good is unimportant or not really valuable. It does suggest, however, that it would be a good idea for us to think again before appealing unreflectively to 'the public/private distinction' in justificatory contexts. . . . Rather, *first* we must ask what this purported distinction is *for*, that is, *why* we want to make it at all. To answer this question will bring us back to some relatively concrete context of human action, probably political action, and it is only in the context of connecting the issue of the public and private to that antecedent potential context of political action that the distinction will make any sense" (*Public Goods*, 106–7).

Bibliography

Administration for Children and Families. *Healthy Marriage Initiative*. 24 June 2008. U.S. Dept. of Health and Human Services. *http://www.acf.hhs.gov/healthymarriage* (accessed 24 March 2009).

Allen, Anita L. *Uneasy Access: Privacy for Women in a Free Society*. Totowa, NJ: Rowman & Littlefield, 1988.

Amato, Paul R. "Institutional, Companionate, and Individualistic Marriage: A Social Psychological Perspective on Marital Change." In *Marriage and Family: Perspectives and Complexities*, edited by H. Elizabeth Peters and Claire Kamp Dush. New York: Columbia University Press, 2009.

Arendt, Hannah. "Reflections on Little Rock." *Dissent* 6, no. 1 (1959): 45–56.

Aristotle. *Nicomachean Ethics*. Translated by Terence Irwin. Indianapolis: Hackett, 1985.

———. *The Politics*. Trans. Carnes Lord. Chicago: University of Chicago Press, 1984.

Arneil, Barbara, Avigail Eisenberg, Monique Deveaux, and Rita Dhamoon. *Sexual Justice/Cultural Justice: Critical Perspectives in Political Theory and Practice*. New York: Routledge, 2007.

Baker v. State of Vermont, 170 Vt. 194; 744 A.2d 864 (1999).

Bell, Duran. "Defining Marriage and Legitimacy." *Current Anthropology* 38 (1997): 237–53.

Bellah, Robert N., Richard Madsen, William Sullivan, Ann Swidler, et al. *The Good Society*. New York: Knopf, 1991.

Bennhold, Katrin. "A Veil Closes France's Door to Citizenship." *New York Times*, 19 July 2008, late edition, A1+.

Berger, Peter L., and Thomas Luckmann. *The Social Construction of Reality: A Treatise in the Sociology of Knowledge*. New York: Doubleday, 1966.

Berlin, Isaiah. *Four Essays on Liberty.* Oxford: Oxford University Press, 1969.

Beyond Conjugality: Recognizing and Supporting Close Personal Relationships. Law Commission of Canada, 2001. *http://dalspace.library .dal.ca/dspace/handle/10222/10257* (accessed 20 July 2009).

Blankenhorn, David. *The Future of Marriage.* New York: Encounter, 2007.

Bloom, Allan D. *The Republic of Plato.* New York: Basic Books, 1991.

Boele-Woelki, Katharina, and Angelika Fuchs, eds. *Legal Recognition of Same-Sex Couples in Europe.* New York: Intersentia, 2003.

Borneman, John. "Until Death Do Us Part: Marriage/Death in Anthropological Discourse." *American Ethnologist* 23 (1996): 215–35.

Bowers v. Hardwick, 48 U.S. 1039 (1986).

Bradford, Laura. "Note: The Counterrevolution: A Critique of Recent Proposals to Reform No-Fault Divorce Laws." *Stanford Law Review* 49 (1997): 607–36.

Brinig, Margaret F. "The Supreme Court's Impact on Marriage, 1967–1990." *Howard Law Journal* 41 (1998): 271–87.

Brown, Wendy. *States of Injury: Power and Freedom in Late Modernity.* Princeton, NJ: Princeton University Press, 1995.

Butler, Melissa. "Early Liberal Roots of Feminism: John Locke and the Attack on Patriarchy." *American Political Science Review* 72, no. 1 (1978): 135–50. Reprinted in *Feminist Interpretations and Political Theory,* edited by Mary Lyndon Shanley and Carole Pateman, 74–94. University Park, PA: Pennsylvania State University Press, 1991.

Cahn, Naomi R. "Family Law, Federalism, and the Federal Courts." *Iowa Law Review* 79 (1994): 1073–1126.

California Domestic Partners Rights and Responsibilities Act. A.B. 205. 22 Sept. 2003.

California Family Code §297–299.6.

Caregiver Assistance and Relief Effort (CARE) *Act.* Senate Bill 2121. 1 Oct. 2007.

Card, Claudia. "Against Marriage and Motherhood." *Hypatia* 11, no. 3 (1996): 1–23.

———. "Gay Divorce: Thoughts on the Legal Regulation of Marriage." *Hypatia* 22, no. 1 (2007): 24–38.

Christensen, Craig. "If Not Marriage? On Securing Gay and Lesbian Family Values by a 'Simulacrum of Marriage.'" *Fordham Law Review* 66 (1998): 1699–1784.

Cook, Thomas I., and Arnaud B. Leavelle. "German Idealism and American Theories of the Democratic Community." *Journal of Politics* 5 (1943): 213–36.

Coontz, Stephanie. *Marriage, a History: From Obedience to Intimacy or How Love Conquered Marriage*. New York: Viking, 2005.

Cornell, Drucilla. *At the Heart of Freedom: Feminism, Sex, and Equality*. Princeton, NJ: Princeton University Press, 1998.

Cott, Nancy F. *Public Vows: A History of Marriage and the Nation*. Cambridge, MA: Harvard University Press, 2000.

Crampton, Thomas. "At a Gay Synagogue, a Rabbi Isn't Fazed by Legalities." *New York Times*, 21 March 2004, late edition, A29+.

Creppell, Ingrid. "Locke on Toleration: The Transformation of Constraint." *Political Theory* 24 (1996): 200–40.

Cruz, David B. "Disestablishing Sex and Gender." *California Law Review* 90 (2002): 997–1086.

————. "'Just Don't Call It Marriage': The First Amendment and Marriage as an Expressive Resource." *Southern California Law Review* 74 (2001): 925–1026.

Defense of Marriage Act. Public Law 104-199 (1996).

Dennis v. United States, 341 U.S. 494 (1951).

Derbyshire, John. "Britney's Wedding." *National Review Online*, 9 Jan. 2004. *http://www.nationalreview.com/derbyshire/derbyshire2004010 90845.asp* (accessed 24 March 2009).

Deveaux, Monique. *Cultural Pluralism and Dilemmas of Justice*. Ithaca, NY: Cornell University Press, 2000.

Duggan, Lisa. "Holy Matrimony!" *The Nation*, 15 Mar. 2004, 14–19.

————. "Queering the State." *Social Text* 39 (1994): 1–14.

Dworkin, Richard. *Freedom's Law: The Moral Reading of the American Constitution*. Cambridge, MA: Harvard University Press, 1996.

————. *Law's Empire*. Cambridge, MA: Belknap-Harvard University Press, 1986.

————. *Taking Rights Seriously*. Cambridge, MA: Harvard University Press, 1978.

Eichner, Maxine. "Marriage and the Elephant: The Liberal Democratic State's Regulation of Intimate Relationships between Adults." University of North Carolina Legal Studies Research Paper No. 898740, 2006. *http://papers.ssrn.com/sol3/papers.cfm?abstract_id=898740* (accessed 24 March 2009).

Eisenstadt v. Baird, 405 U.S. 438 (1972).

Ellman, Ira Mark. "The Theory of Alimony." *California Law Review* 77 (1989): 1–81.

Elshtain, Jean Bethke. "Begging to Differ." Review of *Justice, Gender, and the Family* by Susan Moller Okin and *Making All the Difference* by Martha Minow. *Hastings Center Report* 22, no. 1 (1992): 47–48.

———. "Feminism, Family, and Community." *Dissent* 29 (1982): 442–49.

———. *Public Man, Private Woman: Women in Social and Political Thought.* 2d ed. Princeton, NJ: Princeton University Press, 1981.

England, Paula. "A Gender Perspective on Marriage." In *Marriage and Family: Perspectives and Complexities,* edited by H. Elizabeth Peters and Claire Kamp Dush. New York: Columbia University Press, 2009.

Engster, Daniel. *The Heart of Justice: A Political Theory of Caring.* Oxford: Oxford University Press, 2007.

Eskow, Lisa. "The Ultimate Weapon?: Demythologizing Spousal Rape and Reconceptualizing Its Prosecution." *Stanford Law Review* 48 (1996): 677–709.

Falco, Melanie C. "The Road Not Taken: Using the Eighth Amendment to Strike Down Criminal Punishment for Engaging in Consensual Sexual Acts." *North Carolina Law Review* 82 (2004): 723–58.

Farson, Richard E. *Birthrights.* New York: Macmillan, 1974.

Fineman, Martha Albertson. *The Autonomy Myth: A Theory of Dependency.* New York: The New Press, 2004.

———. *The Illusion of Equality: The Rhetoric and Reality of Divorce Reform.* Chicago: University of Chicago Press, 1991.

———. *The Neutered Mother, the Sexual Family and Other Twentieth-Century Tragedies.* New York: Routledge, 1995.

———. "Why Marriage?" In *Just Marriage,* edited by Mary Lyndon Shanley, 46–51. New Democracy Forum / *Boston Review*: Oxford: Oxford University Press, 2004.

Folbre, Nancy. *The Invisible Heart: Economics and Family Values.* New York: The New Press, 2001.

———. *Valuing Children: Rethinking the Economics of the Family.* The Family and Public Policy. Cambridge, MA: Harvard University Press, 2008.

Frank, Jill. *A Democracy of Distinction*. Chicago: University of Chicago Press, 2005.

Freeman, Michael D. A. *Children's Rights*. 2 vols. Burlington, VT: Ashgate Dartmouth, 2004.

Friedan, Betty. *The Feminine Mystique*. New York: Norton, 1963.

Gallie, W. B. "Essentially Contested Concepts." *Proceedings of the Aristotelian Society* 56 (1956): 167–98.

Galston, William A. "Divorce American Style." *The Public Interest* 124 (1996): 12–17.

———. "Reinstitutionalization of Marriage: Political Theory and Public Policy." In *Promises to Keep: The Decline and Renewal of Marriage in America*, edited by David Popenoe, Jean Bethke Elshtain, and David Blankenhorn, 271–92. Lanham, MD: Rowman and Littlefield, 1996.

Garsten, Bryan. *Saving Persuasion: A Defense of Rhetoric and Judgment*. Cambridge, MA: Harvard University Press, 2006.

Geertz, Clifford. "Religion as a Cultural System." In *The Interpretation of Cultures*, 87–125. New York: Basic Books, 1973.

Geuss, Raymond. *Public Goods, Private Goods*. Princeton, NJ: Princeton University Press, 2003.

Glendon, Mary Ann. *Abortion and Divorce in Western Law*. 1986 Julius Rosenthal Foundation Lectures. Cambridge, MA: Harvard University Press, 1987.

———. *The New Family and the New Property*. Toronto: Butterworths, 1981.

Goodridge v. Dept. of Public Health, 440 Mass. 309 (2003).

Goodstein, Laurie. "Gay Couples Seek Unions in God's Eyes." *New York Times*, 30 Jan. 2004, late edition, A1+.

Gould-Wartofsky, Michael. "Too Cruel for School." *Harvard Crimson*, 18 Oct. 2005. *http://www.thecrimson.com/article.aspx?ref=509189* (accessed 24 March 2009).

Green, Richard. "Griswold's Legacy: Fornication and Adultery as Crimes." *Ohio Northern University Law Review* 16 (1989): 545–49.

Griswold v. Connecticut, 381 U.S. 479 (1965).

Gross, Jane. "Older Women Team Up to Face Future Together." *New York Times*, 27 Feb. 2004, A1, A22.

Grossberg, Michael. *Governing the Hearth: Law and the Family in Nineteenth-Century America*. Chapel Hill: University of North Carolina Press, 1985.

Hafen, Bruce C. "The Constitutional Status of Marriage, Kinship, and Sexual Privacy: Balancing the Individual and Social Interests." *Michigan Law Review* 81 (1983): 463–574.

Hamilton, Carolyn, and Alison Perry, eds. *Family Law in Europe*. London: Butterworths, 2002.

Harris, Leslie J., Lee E. Teitelbaum, and Carol A. Weisbrod. *Family Law*. New York: Aspen Law and Business, 1996.

Hart, H.L.A. *The Concept of Law*. Oxford: Clarendon Press, 1961.

Hartog, Hendrik. *Man and Wife in America: A History*. Cambridge, MA: Harvard University Press, 2000.

Hegel, Georg Wilhelm Friedrich. *Hegel's Philosophy of Right*, translated by T. M. Knox. London: Oxford University Press, 1952.

———. *The Philosophy of History*, translated by J. Sibree. New York: Dover, 1956.

Hirschmann, Nancy J. *Rethinking Obligation: A Feminist Method for Political Theory*. Ithaca, NY: Cornell University Press, 1992.

Horton, Sue. "The Next Same-Sex Challenge: Divorce." *Los Angeles Times*, 24 July 2008. *http://articles.latimes.com/2008/jul/25/local /me-gaydivorce25* (accessed 24 March 2009).

Humboldt, Wilhelm von. *The Limits of State Action*, edited by J. W. Burrow. Cambridge: Cambridge University Press, 1969. Liberty Classics Ed. Indianapolis, IND: Liberty Fund, 1993.

In re Marriage Cases, 43 Cal. 4th 757.

Jefferson, Thomas. "Query XVII: Religion." *Notes on the State of Virginia* (1785). In *The Portable Thomas Jefferson*, edited by Merrill D. Peterson, 208–13. New York: Penguin, 1977.

Johnson, Julia Overturf, Robert Kominski, Kristin Smith, and Paul Tillman. "Changes in the Lives of U.S. Children: 1990–2000." Population Division Working Paper No. 78. U.S. Census Bureau, 2005. http:// www.census.gov/population/www/documentation/twps0078/ twps0078.html (accessed 24 March 2009).

Jones, Cathy J. "The Rights to Marry and Divorce: A New Look at Some Unanswered Questions." *Washington University Law Quarterly* 63 (1985): 577–647.

Karst, Kenneth L. "The Freedom of Intimate Association." *Yale Law Journal* 89 (1980): 624–92.

Kennedy, Shawn G. "Ruling Clouds Inheritance of Rentals." *New York Times*, 20 March 1988, 538.

Kittay, Eva Feder. *Love's Labor: Essays on Women, Equality, and Dependency*. New York: Routledge, 1999.

Knox, Virginia, and David Fein. "Supporting Healthy Marriage: Designing a Marriage Education Demonstration for Low-income Married Couples." In *Marriage and Family: Perspectives and Complexities*, edited by H. Elizabeth Peters and Claire Kamp Dush. New York: Columbia University Press, 2009.

Laslett, Peter. Introduction to John Locke. In *Two Treatises of Government*, edited by P. Laslett, 3–126. Cambridge: Cambridge University Press, 1960.

———. *The World We Have Lost*. London: Methuen, 1965.

Lawrence v. Texas, 539 U.S. 558 (2003).

Leach, Edmund R. "Polyandry, Inheritance and the Definition of Marriage." *Man* 55 (1955): 182–86.

———. *Rethinking Anthropology*. London: Athlone, 1961.

Lehman, Jeffery, and Shirelle Phelps, eds. *West's Encyclopedia of American Law*. Vol. 3. Detroit: Thomson/Gale, 2005.

Lehmann-Haupt, Rachel. "Need a Minister? How about Your Brother?" *New York Times*, 12 Jan. 2003, late edition, sec. 9, 1+.

Lévi-Strauss, Claude. "The Family." In *Man, Culture, and Society*, edited by Harry L. Shapiro, 261–85. New York: Oxford University Press, 1956.

Levy, Traci M. "At the Intersection of Intimacy and Care: Redefining 'Family' through the Lens of a Public Ethic of Care." *Politics and Gender* 1 (2005): 65–95.

Locke, John. *A Letter Concerning Toleration*, edited by James H. Tully. Indianapolis, IN: Hackett, 1983.

———. *The Second Treatise of Government: An Essay concerning the True Original, Extent, and End of Civil Government*. In *Two Treatises of Government*, edited by Peter Laslett, 265–428. Cambridge: Cambridge University Press, 1988.

Loving v. Virginia, 388 U.S. 1, 12 (1967).

MacFarlane, Alan. *Marriage and Love in England: Modes of Reproduction, 1300–1840*. New York: Blackwell, 1986.

———. *The Origins of English Individualism: The Family, Property, and Social Transition*. Cambridge: Cambridge University Press, 1978.

MacKinnon, Catharine A. *Feminism Unmodified: Discourse on Life and Law*. Cambridge, MA: Harvard University Press, 1987.

Madison, James. "Memorial and Remonstrance against Religious Assessments" (1785). In *James Madison on Religious Liberty*, edited by Robert Alley, 21–38. Buffalo, NY: Prometheus, 1985.

Mankiw, N. Gregory. *Principles of Macroeconomics*. 4th ed. Mason, OH: Thomson South-Western, 2007.

Maynard v. Hill, 125 U.S. 190 (1888).

McClain, Linda C. *The Place of Families: Fostering Capacity, Equality, and Responsibility*. Cambridge, MA: Harvard University Press, 2006.

McKinley, Jesse. "Same-Sex Marriages Begin in California." *New York Times*, 17 June 2008. http://www.nytimes.com/2008/06/17/us/17weddings.html (accessed 24 March 2009).

Metz, Tamara. "The Liberal Case for Disestablishing Marriage." *Contemporary Political Theory* 6 (2007): 196–217.

Meyer v. Nebraska, 262 U.S. 390 (1923).

Michels, Spencer. "Same-Sex Couples Begin Marrying in California." *Online NewsHour*. Public Broadcasting Service, 17 June 2008. http://www.pbs.org/newshour/bb/law/jan-june08/justmarried_06-17.html (accessed 24 March 2009)

Mill, John Stuart. "Early Essay on Marriage and Divorce." In *Essays on Sex Equality: John Stuart Mill and Harriet Taylor Mill*, edited by Alice S. Rossi, 67–84. Chicago: University of Chicago Press, 1970.

———. *On Liberty. Mill: Texts and Commentaries*, edited by Alan Ryan, 41–131. Norton Critical Ed. New York: Norton, 1997.

———. *The Subjection of Women*. In *Essays on Sex Equality: John Stuart Mill and Harriet Taylor Mill*, edited by Alice S. Rossi, 123–242. Chicago: University of Chicago Press, 1970.

Miller, Jean Baker. *Toward a New Psychology of Women*. Boston: Beacon, 1986.

Minow, Martha. "Rights and Relations: Families and Children." *Making All the Difference: Inclusion, Exclusion, and American Law*. Ithaca, NY: Cornell University Press, 1990.

———. "Rights for the Next Generation: A Feminist Approach to Children's Rights." *Harvard Women's Law Journal* 9, no. 1 (1986): 1–24.

Minow, Martha, and Mary Lyndon Shanley. "Relational Rights and Responsibilities: Revisioning the Family in Liberal Political Theory and Law." *Hypatia* 11, no. 1 (1996): 4–29.

Morriss, Peter. "How to Think About Marriage: Autonomy, Equality, Recognition." *Irish Political Studies* 22 (2007): 545–64.

New Hampshire House Bill 437-FN-LOCAL. 1 Jan. 2008.

Nock, Steven L. "The Future of Marriage." In *Marriage and Family: Perspectives and Complexities*, edited by H. Elizabeth Peters and Claire Kamp Dush. New York: Columbia University Press, 2009.

Noddings, Nel. *Caring: A Feminine Approach to Ethics and Moral Education*. Berkeley: University of California Press, 1984.

Noel v. Ewing, 9 Ind. 36 (1857).

Nussbaum, Martha. *Sex and Social Justice*. New York: Oxford University Press, 1999.

Okin, Susan Moller. "Humanist Liberalism." In *Liberalism and the Moral Life*, edited by Nancy Rosenblum. Cambridge, MA: Harvard University Press, 1989.

———. *Is Multiculturalism Bad for Women?* Edited by Joshua Cohen, Matthew Howard, and Martha C. Nussbaum. Princeton, NJ: Princeton University Press, 1999.

———. *Justice, Gender, and the Family*. New York: Basic Books, 1989.

———. "Political Liberalism: Book Review." *The American Political Science Review* 87 (1993): 1010–11.

———. "Reason and Feeling in Thinking about Justice." *Ethics* 99 (1989): 229–49.

———. *Women in Western Political Thought*. Princeton, NJ: Princeton University Press, 1979.

Olsen, Frances E. "The Family and the Market: A Study of Ideology and Legal Reform." *Harvard Law Review* 96 (1983): 1497–1578.

———. "The Myth of State Intervention in the Family." *University of Michigan Journal of Law Reform* 18 (1984–85): 835.

Olsen, Glenn W. *Christian Marriage: A Historical Study*. New York: Crossroad, 2001.

Opinions of the Justices to the Senate, 440 Mass. 1201 (2004).

Pateman, Carole. *The Disorder of Women: Democracy, Feminism, and Political Theory*. Stanford, CA: Stanford University Press, 1989.

———. *The Sexual Contract*. Stanford, CA: Stanford University Press, 1988.

Peters, H. Elizabeth, and Claire Kamp Dush, eds. *Marriage and Family: Perspectives and Complexities*. New York: Columbia University Press, 2009.

Pettit, Philip. *Republicanism: A Theory of Freedom and Government.* New York: Oxford University Press, 1999.

Posner, Richard A., and Katharine B. Silbaugh. *A Guide to America's Sex Laws.* Chicago: University of Chicago Press, 1996.

Purdy, Laura. *In Their Best Interests?: The Case against Equal Rights for Children.* Ithaca, NY: Cornell University Press, 1992.

Rauch, Jonathan. "Family Reunion: The Case against the Case against Gay Marriage." *Democracy: A Journal of Ideas* 5 (2007). Review of *The Future of Marriage* by David Blankenhorn. http://www.democracyjournal.org/article.php?ID=6539 (accessed 24 March 2009).

Rawls, John. *Justice as Fairness: A Restatement.* Edited by Erin Kelly. Cambridge, MA: Belknap-Harvard University Press, 2001.

———. "Justice as Fairness: Political Not Metaphysical." *Philosophy and Public Affairs* 14 (1985): 223–251.

———. *Law of Peoples, with "The Idea of Public Reason Revisited."* Cambridge, MA: Harvard University Press, 1999.

———. *Political Liberalism.* New York: Columbia University Press, 1993.

———. *A Theory of Justice.* Cambridge, MA: Harvard University Press, 1971.

Regan, Milton C., Jr. *Family Law and the Pursuit of Intimacy.* New York: New York University Press, 1993.

Reynolds v. United States, 98 U.S. 145 (1878).

Rich, Adrienne. "Compulsory Heterosexuality and Lesbian Existence." *Signs* 5 (1980): 631–60.

Robson, C. B. "Francis Lieber's Theories of Society, Government, and Liberty." *Journal of Politics* 4 (1942): 227–49.

Rowe, Gretchen, Mary Murphy, and Meghan Williamson. *Welfare Rules Databook: State TANF Policies as of July 2005.* Washington, DC: Urban Institute, 2006.

Ryan, Alan. "Liberalism." In *A Companion to Contemporary Political Philosophy*, edited by Robert Goodin and Philip Pettit, 291–311. Oxford, UK: Blackwell, 1995.

Ryan, Rebecca M. "The Sex Right: A Legal History of the Marital Rape Exemption." *Law and Social Inquiry* 20 (1995): 941–1001.

Sandel, Michael J. *Democracy's Discontent: America in Search of a Public Philosophy.* Cambridge, MA: Belknap/Harvard University Press, 1996.

Scalia, Antonin. *A Matter of Interpretation: Federal Courts and the Law.* Princeton, NJ: Princeton University Press, 1997.

Schenck v. United States, 249 U.S. 47 (1919).

Schneider, Carl E. "The Channeling Function in Family Law." *Hofstra Law Review* 20 (1992): 495–532.

———. "Marriage, Morals, and the Law: No-Fault Divorce and Moral Discourse." *Utah Law Review* 2 (1994): 503–85.

———. "Moral Discourse and the Transformation of American Family Law." *Michigan Law Review* 83 (1985): 1803–79.

Scott, Elizabeth S. "Rational Decisionmaking in Marriage and Divorce." *Virginia Law Review* 76 (1990): 9–94.

Shachar, Ayelet. *Multicultural Jurisdictions: Cultural Difference and Women's Rights.* Cambridge: Cambridge University Press, 2001.

Shanley, Mary Lyndon. *Just Marriage.* New Democracy Forum / *Boston Review*; Oxford: Oxford University Press, 2004.

———. "Just Marriage: On the Public Importance of Private Unions." *Boston Review* 28, nos. 3–5 (Summer 2003): 19–23.

———. "Marital Slavery and Friendship: John Stuart Mill's *The Subjection of Women.*" *Political Theory* 9 (1981): 229–47.

———. "Marriage Contract and Social Contract in Seventeenth-Century English Political Thought." *Western Political Quarterly* 32 (1979): 79–91. Revised and reprinted in *The Family in Political Thought*, edited by Jean Bethke Elshtain, 80–95. Amherst: University of Massachusetts Press, 1982.

Shell, Susan. "The Liberal Case against Gay Marriage." *The Public Interest* 156 (2004): 3–15.

Shklar, Judith N. "The Liberalism of Fear." In *Liberalism and the Moral Life*, edited by Nancy Rosenblum, 21–38. Cambridge, MA: Harvard University Press, 1989. Reprinted in *Political Thought and Political Thinkers*, edited by Stanley Hoffmann, 3–20. Chicago: University of Chicago Press, 1998.

———. "What Is the Use of Utopia?" In *Heterotopia: Postmodern Utopia and the Body Politic*, edited by Tobin Siebers, 40–57. Ann Arbor, MI: University of Michigan Press, 1994. Reprinted in *Political Thought and Political Thinkers*, edited by Stanley Hoffman, 75–90. Chicago: University of Chicago Press, 1998.

Shultz, Marjorie Maguire. "Contractual Ordering of Marriage: A New Model for State Policy." *California Law Review* 70 (1982): 204–334.

Simmons, Tavia, and Grace O'Neill. *Households and Families: 2000.* Census 2000 Brief 01-8. U. S. Census Bureau, 2001. http://www.census.gov/population/www/cen2000/briefs.html (accessed 24 March 2009).

Singer, Jana B. "The Privatization of Family Law." *Wisconsin Law Review* (1992): 1443–1567.

Skinner, Quentin. "The Idea of Negative Liberty: Philosophical and Historical Perspectives." *Philosophy in History: Essays on the Historiography of Philosophy,* edited by Richard Rorty, J. B. Schneewind, and Quentin Skinner, 193–223. Cambridge: Cambridge University Press, 1984.

Skinner v. Oklahoma ex rel. Williamson, 316 U.S. 535 (1942).

Smith, Anna Marie. *Welfare Reform and Sexual Regulation.* Cambridge: Cambridge University Press: 2007.

Spinner-Halev, Jeff. *Surviving Diversity: Religion and Democratic Citizenship.* Baltimore, MD: The Johns Hopkins University Press, 2000.

Stacey, Judith. "Toward Equal Regard for Marriages and Other Imperfect IntimateAffiliations." *Hofstra Law Review* 32 (2003): 331–48.

Steinberger, Peter. *The Concept of Political Judgment.* Chicago: University of Chicago Press, 1993.

Stevenson's Heirs v. Sullivant, 18 U.S. (5 Wheat.) 207 (1820).

Stone, Lawrence. *Road to Divorce: England 1530–1987.* Oxford: Oxford University Press, 1990.

Strassberg, Maura I. "Distinctions of Form or Substance: Monogamy, Polygamy and Same-Sex Marriage." *North Carolina Law Review* 75 (1997): 1501–1624.

Strauss, Leo. *Natural Right and History.* Charles R. Walgreen Foundation Lectures. Chicago: University of Chicago Press, 1950.

———. "Political Philosophy and History." *What Is Political Philosophy and Other Studies,* 56–77. Chicago: University of Chicago Press, 1959.

Sugarman, Stephen D., and Herma Hill Kay, eds. *Divorce Reform at the Crossroads.* New Haven, CT: Yale University Press, 1990.

Taylor, Charles. *Multiculturalism and "The Politics of Recognition."* Princeton, NJ: Princeton University Press, 1992.

Taylor (Mill), Harriet. "Early Essay on Marriage and Divorce." In *Essays on Sex Equality: John Stuart Mill and Harriet Taylor Mill,* edited by Alice S. Rossi, 84–87. Chicago: University of Chicago Press, 1970.

Thornton, Arland. "Comparative and Historical Perspectives on Marriage, Divorce, and Family Life." *Utah Law Review* 1994, no. 2 (1994): 587–604.

Traer, James F. *Marriage and the Family in Eighteenth-Century France.* Ithaca, NY: Cornell University Press, 1980.

Tronto, Joan C. *Moral Boundaries: A Political Argument for an Ethic of Care.* New York: Routledge, 1993.

Tully, James. "Political Philosophy as a Critical Activity." *What is Political Theory?*, 80–102. London: Sage, 2004.

Universal Life Church Monastery. http://www.ulcordination.org (accessed 24 March 2009).

Utah v. Green, 2001 UT App 131.

Utah v. Holm, 2006 UT 31 (2006).

Van Parijs, Philippe. *Real Freedom for All: What (If Anything) Can Justify Capitalism?* Oxford: Clarendon, 1995.

Varney, Sarah. "Octogenarian Gay-Rights Pioneers Wed in California." *All Things Considered.* Natl. Public Radio, 17 June 2008. http://www.npr.org/templates/story/story.php?storyId=91606620 (accessed 24 March 2009).

Wade v. Kalbfleisch, 58 N.Y. 282 (1874).

Waite, Linda J., and Maggie Gallagher. *The Case for Marriage.* New York: Doubleday, 2000.

Waldman, Steven. "Rick Warren's Controversial Comments on Gay Marriage." Interview with Rick Warren. *Beliefnet*, 17 Dec. 2008. http://blog.beliefnet.com/stevenwaldman/2008/12/rick-warrens-controversial-com.html (accessed 24 March 2009).

Walzer, Michael. *Spheres of Justice: A Defense of Pluralism and Equality.* New York: Basic Books, 1983.

Warner, Michael. *The Trouble with Normal: Sex, Politics, and the Ethics of Queer Life.* Cambridge, MA: Harvard University Press, 1999.

Warren, Rick. Transcript: The Rev. Rick Warren's Invocation. *Los Angeles Times*, 21 Jan. 2009. http://www.latimes.com/news/politics/la-na-inaug-warren-prayer-text21-2009jan21,0,2894094.story (accessed 24 March 2009).

Weitzman, Lenore J. *The Divorce Revolution: The Unexpected Social and Economic Consequences for Women and Children in America.* New York: Free, 1985.

Weitzman, Lenore J. "Legal Regulation of Marriage: Tradition and Change." *California Law Review* 62 (1974): 1169–1288.

Wood, Gordon S. *The Radicalism of the American Revolution.* New York: Knopf, 1992.

Zablocki v. Redhail, 434 U.S. 374 (1978).

Zelig, Kaylah Campos. "Putting Responsibility Back into Marriage: Making a Case for Mandatory Prenuptials." *University of Colorado Law Review* 64 (1993): 1223–45.

Index

action, 134; as affected by belief, 91–
94, 96, 106, 116, 120, 142–43, 146,
178n3; as appropriate object of state
regulation, 8, 26–27, 35, 41, 69,
115, 151, 159–60; as basis for consensus, 136; and instrumental theory
of law, 91–94; and limited liberal
account of marriage, 20, 25–28;
Locke on, 118, 127, Mill on, 69–70;
as part of social institution, 86,
95–97, 99
adultery, 164n11
adults, 181n34; care among, 61, 126,
132, 140; contracts between, 51, 72,
139; in ICGUs, 138; nonsexually
intimate, 121
antimiscegenation laws, 168n30
Arendt, Hannah, 125
Aristotle, 160, 179n20
authority: divine, 54, 57–59, 63;
ethical, 11, 86–87, 101–8, 114–16,
118–19, 134, 142–43; problem
of, 114–19, 141; public, 4, 10, 11,
23, 30–32, 58, 69, 99, 100, 102–3,
104, 106, 115, 144, 182n57; —as
distinct from state, 106, 144–46;
religious, 4, 5, 7, 59, 109, 110,
119, 134, 143, 144, 145; secular, 4,
109–10, 145, 146; state 4, 10–11,
30, 31–32, 55, 58, 69, 71, 97,
106, 107, 115, 116, 118, 119, 141,
142, 144
autonomy: of groups, 154–55, 158; of
individuals, 125–126, 154, 158,
167n5, 175n25

Baker v. State of Vermont, 33–37, 89
baptism, 114–15, 117, 120, 150
bar mitzvah, 114–15, 119, 141
Berlin, Isaiah, 5, 165n22
Beyond Conjugality, 15
Bowers v. Hardwick, 179n16, 182n52

California, Supreme Court of. See *In
re Marriage Cases*
Card, Claudia, 88, 95, 97, 99, 101,
175n22
care. *See* intimate care
caregivers, 13, 74–77, 80, 126, 131;
disadvantages to unwed, 181n31;
inequality among, 128–29; public
support for, 77, 147
childrearing, 41, 48, 56, 59, 121,
171n38
children, 61, 72, 79, 129, 139, 172n57,
181n34; abuse of, 123, 137; adult,
121; census statistics on, 179n13;
rights of, 138–39; state's responsibility to, 60, 62, 68–70, 77, 80, 82,
109, 131, 178n38. *See also* parent-
child relationship; parents
civil unions, 9, 34–35, 89–90, 94–95,
98, 103, 105–6, 108, 111, 114, 130,
141, 181n32; as parallel-status regime, 38–39, 44. *See also* domestic
partnership; intimate caregiving
union status
cohabitation, 121–22. *See also*
families: nonmarital; intimate care
community: alternative, 177n42;
Hegel on, 100–107, 176n28; Locke
on, 49, 54; and marriage, 24, 54, 92,

public discourse, 49, 124, 128, 129, 136, 140
public policy, 4, 7, 15–16, 19, 130, 153; and intimate care, 131, 135, 140, 149; target problem of, 128–29, 137, 141. *See also* family policy; state action
public recognition, 30, 31, 40, 47, 58, 86, 98–107, 110, 142, 145; function of, 11, 13, 14, 33–34, 41, 100, 115–17
public sphere, 6, 69, 74–76, 105, 142, 155, 157. *See also* public/private distinction
public-welfare goals, 3, 5, 14, 48, 88, 134, 148

queer theory, 10, 96, 165n24

Rauch, Jonathan, 93, 133
Rawls, John, 5, 19, 77, 147, 165n21, 169n1, 174n2
reciprocity, 13, 60, 65, 122, 132–33, 135, 155
relationships. *See* intimate caregiving relationships
religion, 7, 32, 50, 54, 57, 130, 143, 177n33; as formal comprehensive social institution, 9, 12, 87, 106, 119; freedom of, 25–26, 30, 40, 41, 53, 155, 159; Locke on, 57, 59; (non)establishment of, 11, 113–14, 118, 141, 150, 163n4
Reynolds v. United States, 25–28, 30, 93, 111, 167nn7–9
rights, 23, 63, 141, 149, 154; of children, 138–39; and contract, 32, 53; as a liberal value, 6, 16, 20, 21, 25, 29, 48; of marriage, 22, 28–32, 38–43, 45, 169n46; positive, 29–30, 32, 39–40; of privacy, 31, 39. *See also* freedom
Schenck v. United States, 173n61
Schneider, Carl, 88, 95–96, 99, 101, 175n17

secularism. *See under* authority
self-understanding, 11, 86, 92–94, 101, 106, 108, 111, 115–16, 148, 159. *See also* status, constitutive
Shanley, Mary Lyndon, 52, 73, 90, 131, 133, 170nn5, 10, and 14
Shklar, Judith, 6, 155, 159, 161, 169n2, 179n19
single persons, 31, 140, 183n60; "single-person's worry," 149–50
Skinner v. Oklahoma, 168n20
Smith, Anna Marie, 125, 164n12, 182n42
Social Security. *See* welfare
stability, 6, 7, 13, 16, 157, 158
state: Hegel on, 106–7; in liberal theory, 6–8, 17, 29, 30, 35, 48, 49, 51; as public authority (*see under* authority). *See also* limited government; state action
state action: constitutive purposes of, 100–107, 109, 111, 120, 178n3; Humboldt on, 67–68, 70, 72, 172n57; instrumental purposes of, 36, 53, 59–60, 71, 76–78, 115–16, 127–28, 134–35, 137, 143–146, 148–49, 159–60; and intimate care, 60–62, 69–71, 72, 74, 120, 124, 127, 135–37, 140, 149, 155; in jurisprudence, 28, 30–32, 37–41; justifications for, 13–14, 27, 30, 48, 79, 80–81, 137–38; in liberal theory, 6–8, 17, 29, 35, 41, 43, 72; Locke on, 53–58, 60, 62, 81–82, 116–18, 151; Mill on, 64–66, 69–72, 108–9; and public/private distinction, 53–55, 68–69, 117–18, 125, 155, 158; reach and limits of, 13, 16, 20, 24, 36, 44, 74, 76–77, 80, 117, 120, 148, 155, 158–60, 161. *See also* authority; family; family policy; freedom; marriage; public policy
status, 42, 49, 82; constitutive, 36–37, 45, 58, 71, 89–92, 96–97, 105–6, 108, 111, 115, 116, 119, 133, 134,